The Story of Human Language
Parts I–III
John McWhorter, Ph.D.

PUBLISHED BY:

THE TEACHING COMPANY
4840 Westfields Boulevard, Suite 500
Chantilly, Virginia 20151-2299
1-800-TEACH-12
Fax—703-378-3819
www.teach12.com

Copyright © The Teaching Company, 2004

Printed in the United States of America

This book is in copyright. All rights reserved.

Without limiting the rights under copyright reserved above,
no part of this publication may be reproduced, stored in
or introduced into a retrieval system, or transmitted,
in any form, or by any means
(electronic, mechanical, photocopying, recording, or otherwise),
without the prior written permission of
The Teaching Company.

John McWhorter, Ph.D.
Senior Fellow in Public Policy, Manhattan Institute

John McWhorter, Senior Fellow at the Manhattan Institute, earned his Ph.D. in linguistics from Stanford University in 1993 and became Associate Professor of Linguistics at UC Berkeley after teaching at Cornell University. His academic specialty is language change and language contact. He is the author of *The Power of Babel: A Natural History of Language*, on how the world's languages arise, change, and mix. He has also written a book on dialects and Black English, *The Word on the Street*. His books on creoles include *Language Change and Language Contact in Pidgins and Creoles*, *The Missing Spanish Creoles*, and an anthology of his creole articles called *Defining Creole*. Beyond his work in linguistics, Dr. McWhorter is the author of *Losing the Race* and an anthology of race writings, *Authentically Black*. He has written on race and cultural issues for *The New Republic*, *The Wall Street Journal*, *The Washington Post*, *The Chronicle of Higher Education*, *The National Review*, *The Los Angeles Times*, *The American Enterprise*, and *The New York Times*. Dr. McWhorter has appeared on *Dateline NBC*, *Politically Incorrect*, *Talk of the Nation*, *Today*, *Good Morning, America*, *The Jim Lehrer NewsHour*, and *Fresh Air* and does regular commentaries for *All Things Considered*. His latest book is *Doing Our Own Thing: The Degradation of Language and Music in America and Why We Should, Like, Care*.

Table of Contents
The Story of Human Language

Professor Biography		 i
Course Scope		 1
Lecture One	What Is Language?... 3
Lecture Two	When Language Began 9
Lecture Three	How Language Changes—Sound Change 14
Lecture Four	How Language Changes— Building New Material.................................... 20
Lecture Five	How Language Changes— Meaning and Order 27
Lecture Six	How Language Changes— Many Directions... 32
Lecture Seven	How Language Changes— Modern English.. 37
Lecture Eight	Language Families—Indo-European 41
Lecture Nine	Language Families— Tracing Indo-European 47
Lecture Ten	Language Families— Diversity of Structures 52
Lecture Eleven	Language Families—Clues to the Past............ 57
Lecture Twelve	The Case Against the World's First Language.............................. 62
Lecture Thirteen	The Case For the World's First Language 67
Lecture Fourteen	Dialects—Subspecies of Species 71
Lecture Fifteen	Dialects—Where Do You Draw the Line? 77
Lecture Sixteen	Dialects—Two Tongues in One Mouth 82
Lecture Seventeen	Dialects—The Standard as Token of the Past 86
Lecture Eighteen	Dialects—Spoken Style, Written Style 90
Lecture Nineteen	Dialects—The Fallacy of Blackboard Grammar................................... 96
Lecture Twenty	Language Mixture—Words 101

Table of Contents
The Story of Human Language

Lecture Twenty-One	Language Mixture—Grammar	106
Lecture Twenty-Two	Language Mixture—Language Areas	111
Lecture Twenty-Three	Language Develops Beyond the Call of Duty	115
Lecture Twenty-Four	Language Interrupted	120
Lecture Twenty-Five	A New Perspective on the Story of English	126
Lecture Twenty-Six	Does Culture Drive Language Change?	130
Lecture Twenty-Seven	Language Starts Over—Pidgins	135
Lecture Twenty-Eight	Language Starts Over—Creoles I	140
Lecture Twenty-Nine	Language Starts Over—Creoles II	145
Lecture Thirty	Language Starts Over—Signs of the New	150
Lecture Thirty-One	Language Starts Over—The Creole Continuum	154
Lecture Thirty-Two	What Is Black English?	159
Lecture Thirty-Three	Language Death—The Problem	163
Lecture Thirty-Four	Language Death—Prognosis	166
Lecture Thirty-Five	Artificial Languages	170
Lecture Thirty-Six	Finale—Master Class	174
Language Maps		179
Timeline		184
Glossary		185
Bibliography		194

The Story of Human Language

Scope:

There are 6,000 languages in the world, in so much variety that many languages would leave English speakers wondering just how a human being could possibly learn and use them. How did these languages come to be? Why isn't there just a single language?

This course answers these questions. Like animals and plants, the world's languages are the result of a long "natural history," which began with a single first language spoken in Africa. As human populations migrated to new places on the planet, each group's version of the language changed in different ways, until there were several languages where there was once one. Eventually, there were thousands.

Languages change in ways that make old sounds into new sounds and words into grammar, and they shift in different directions, so that eventually there are languages as different as German and Japanese. At all times, any language is gradually on its way to changing into a new one; the language that is not gradually turning upside-down is one on the verge of extinction.

This kind of change is so relentless that it even creates "languages within languages." In separate populations who speak the same language, changes differ. The result is variations upon the language—that is, dialects. Often one dialect is chosen as the standard one, and when it is used in writing, it changes more slowly than the ones that are mostly just spoken, because the permanency of writing has an official look that makes change seem suspicious. But the dialects that are mostly just spoken keep on changing at a more normal pace.

Then, the languages of the world tend to mix together on various levels. All languages borrow words from one another; there is no "pure" vocabulary. But some borrow so much vocabulary that there is little original material left, such as in English. And meanwhile, languages spoken alongside one another also trade grammar, coming to look alike the way married couples sometimes do. Some languages are even direct crosses between one language and another, two languages having "reproduced" along the lines of mitosis.

Ordinarily, language change is an exuberant process that makes languages develop far more machinery than they need—the gender markers in such languages as French and German are hardly necessary to communication, for example. But this overgrowth is checked when history gets in the way. For example, when people learn a language quickly without being explicitly taught, they develop a pidgin version of it; then, if they need to use this pidgin on an everyday basis, it becomes a real language, called a *creole*. Creoles are language starting again in a fashion—immediately they divide into dialects, mix with other languages, and start building up the decorations that older languages have.

Just as there is an extinction crisis among many of the world's animals and plants, it is estimated that 5,500 of the world's languages will no longer be spoken in 2100. Globalization and urbanization tend to bring people toward one of a few dozen politically dominant languages, and once a generation is not raised in a language, it no longer survives except in writing—if linguists have gotten to it yet. As a language dies, it passes through a "pidgin" stage on its way to expiration. This course, then, is both a celebration and a memorial of a fascinating variety of languages that is unlikely to exist for much longer.

Lecture One
What Is Language?

Scope: Language is more than words; it is also how the words are put together—grammar. The ability to use fluent, nuanced language is local to humans: bees, parrots, and chimps can approximate it but not with the complexity or spontaneity that comes naturally to us. Despite influential speculations, it is unclear whether Neanderthals could speak in the same manner as *Homo sapiens*, and theories that language emerged as the result of a single gene mutation about 30,000 years ago are increasingly controversial as well.

Outline

I. Language is more than words.
   A. By *language*, we do not mean solely words, but the grammar that we use to put them together to produce utterances that reflect our impressions of our lives, experiences, and environment, as well as enable us to affect people and events around us.
   B. One can learn hundreds of words in a foreign language and still be unable to manage even a simple conversation or even say, "You might as well finish it" or "It happened to be on a Tuesday."

II. Communication among lower animals is not "language" in the human sense.
   A. The philosopher Bertrand Russell once wrote, "A dog cannot relate his autobiography; however eloquently he may bark, he cannot tell you that his parents were honest though poor."
   B. Bees.
      1. *How bees "talk."* A bee tells the hive about honey it has found by doing certain dances. In one, the bee moves in a straight line in the direction that the honey is in and waggles its behind with a frequency corresponding to how far away the honey is and with a "liveliness" corresponding to how rich the source is.
      2. *Is this "language"?* But bees only communicate in this manner about the location of food. They cannot chew the fat.

III. Apes' language ability.
  A. Apes seem eerily "like us," and this includes their ability to communicate with us on certain levels. In his famously colloquial, quotidian diary, Samuel Pepys, man of affairs of Restoration England, wrote:

  It is a great baboone, but so like a man in most things, that… yet I cannot believe but that it is a monster got of a man and she-baboone. I do believe it already understands much english; and I am of the mind it might be taught to speak or make signs. (Latham, R.C., and W. Matthews, eds. *The Diary of Samuel Pepys*, Vol. 2. Berkeley: University of California Press, 1970.)

  B. *Early attempts to teach apes language.* In actuality, when people have tried to teach chimpanzees to talk, the results have been limited. In 1909, one chimp learned to say *mama*. In 1916, an orangutan learned to say *papa* and *cup*. In the 1940s, another chimp learned to say *papa*, *mama*, *cup*, and sometimes *up*.

  C. *Apes and sign language.* More recently, researchers have tried to teach chimpanzees sign language. The results have been somewhat more successful.
   1. Starting in 1966, Washoe, at about a year old, took three months to make her first signs, and by four, she had 132 signs.
   2. She could extend *open* from referring to a door to opening containers and turning on faucets, and she once signed *water bird* when a swan passed. She could even put a few words together into "sentences," such as *you me out* for "Let's go out."

  D. *Ape language versus human language.* But these chimpanzees are not using "language" in the human sense.
   1. *Inconsistency.* They tend to respond properly to strings of two or more words only most of the time rather than all of the time.
   2. *Grammar or context?* Some researchers have argued that understanding these strings of words shows that chimpanzees are using "grammar" in the sense of subject versus object and so on. But the correspondence between the words and the immediate context generally makes the meaning of the string clear without any sense of "grammar." One ape knew that *cooler sour cream put* meant, "Put the sour cream in the

cooler," but obviously, this was the only rational meaning those words used together could have.
   3. *Imitation versus communication.* One ape signed along with humans while they were communicating with him 40 percent of the time, while children overlap with adults speaking to them only about 5 percent of the time. This suggests that chimpanzees are imitating more than speaking on their own.
  E. *What is missing from apes' language?* The linguist Charles Hockett listed 13 features of language in the human sense. Among them, what is missing from chimpanzees' (and other creatures') communication are:
   1. *Displacement*: communicating about things and concepts beyond the immediate context and urgency (an animal cannot tell its fellow animals about the giant squid carcass it saw washed up on the beach).
   2. *Productivity*: being able to combine the basic elements of language in infinite combinations (as opposed to restricting communication to a small array of requests for food or announcements of where food is).
IV. Animals do not communicate spontaneously.
  A. *Initiation.* Chimpanzees do not usually initiate a conversation, except to indicate what they want and within a narrow range of activities, such as eating. Washoe's comment on the swan was a once-off surprise.
  B. *Parrots.* Irene Pepperberg (professor of psychology at Brandeis) has trained an African grey parrot named Alex since the late 1970s to answer such questions as "What object is green and three-cornered?," to count things up to six, to ask for food in such sentences as "Want a nut," and even to put names to sounds. Once, asking for a nut each time after being asked questions to name sounds, he slit his eyes and said, "Want a nut—nn, uh, tuh."
   1. But language is largely a trick to Alex: asked what color something is, he will often give every color but the right one, showing intelligence but not a sense of language as communication rather than trick.
   2. He also answers questions with only 80 percent accuracy, because he gets bored; language is a game, not a mode of expression.

- C. *In nature, in the lab.* No apes sign in the wild; no parrots communicate in the wild.
V. When did human language arise?
- A. *Cro-Magnons spoke; Neanderthals grunted?* One hypothesis is that the ability to use language is one of the distinguishing features of *Homo sapiens* as a species.
  1. Philip Lieberman (professor of cognitive and linguistic science at Brown) has argued that the human larynx sits lower in the throat than in animals and that this positioning allows a long, large oral cavity that makes speaking physically possible. He has supported this argument by noting that children, apes, and crucially, Neanderthals do not have the lowered larynx.
  2. This hypothesis is controversial; however, the larynx lowers only at puberty, long after people speak. There is evidence that Neanderthals' larynxes may not have been especially low, and researchers in France have constructed a model oral cavity with a raised larynx that was capable of producing a full range of human speech sounds.
- B. The "Big Bang" observation.
  1. *"Really human."* Actually, although our species emerged about 150,000 years ago, according to paleontological and genetic evidence, many have argued that it was only about 50,000 years ago that there was an explosion in sophistication among *Homo sapiens*, resulting in finer tools, cave art, the bow, tents, and huts.
  2. *Rationale for the "Big Bang" thesis.* Advocates of this argument note that the first species of the genus *Homo* emerged about 2 million years ago; that by 500,000 years ago, human brains were as big as those in modern humans; and that by 100,000 years ago, Neanderthals' brains were even bigger than ours. Yet these scholars observe that during this time, there was only minor cultural development. Remains of humans in Zhoukoudian, China, from 500,000 years ago over the next 300,000 years show no cultural development. According to University of Hawaii linguist and language evolution specialist Derek Bickerton, these humans: "sat for 0.3 million years in the drafty, smoky caves of Zhoukoudian,

cooking bats over smoldering embers and waiting for the caves to fill up with their own garbage" (Bickerton, Derek. *Language and Human Behavior*. Seattle: University of Washington Press, 1995). This has suggested to many that a genetic mutation created the ability for language a good 100,000 years after *Homo sapiens* emerged.

3. *The bigger picture*. However, recent evidence reveals a great deal of sophisticated mental activity, similar to that discovered in Europe, among humans in Africa much further in the past. This suggests that our mental evolution was a gradual process tracing back as far as earlier species, such as *Homo erectus*. It also lends a solution to the problem that the "Big Bang" thesis leaves: if sophistication was achieved in Europe only 50,000 years ago while other humans had already reached Australia by 70,000 years ago, then how did this mental leap—including language—diffuse throughout the world?

C. *Conclusion*. It is highly likely that human language emerged in Africa, with the emergence of either *Homo sapiens* or possibly earlier species of *Homo*. Supporting this is the fact that there is a gene called FOXP2 that is connected with the ability to use language, and it traces back 100,000 years, long before the 50,000-year mark that "Big Bang" theorists designate as the birth of language.

Essential Reading:

Bickerton, Derek. *Language and Human Behavior*. Seattle: University of Washington Press, 1995.

———. *Language and Species*. Chicago: University of Chicago Press, 1990.

Crystal, David. *The Cambridge Encyclopedia of Language*. Cambridge: Cambridge University Press, 1987 (chapter 64: "Language and Other Communication Systems," pp. 396–403).

Oppenheimer, Stephen. *The Real Eve: Modern Man's Journey out of Africa*. New York: Carroll & Graf, 2003.

Supplementary Reading:

Cavalli-Sforza, Luigi Luca, and Francesco Cavalli-Sforza. *The Great Human Diasporas*. Cambridge, MA: Perseus Books, 1995.

Hockett, Charles F. "The Origin of Speech." *Scientific American* 203 (September 1960).

Pepperberg, Irene Maxine. *The Alex Studies: Cognitive and Communicative Abilities of Grey Parrots*. Cambridge, MA: Harvard University Press, 2002.

Wallman, Joel. *Aping Language*. Cambridge: Cambridge University Press, 1992.

Questions to Consider:

1. We often feel that we can "talk" to our pets; dogs can commonly even learn as many as 20 words. But there is a difference between a conversation with a human and one with a cat. What aspects of language are missing in communication with a dog, cat, or parrot?

2. To get a sense of what a marvelously subtle instrument a human language is, think of a foreigner you know who speaks English decently but still makes mistakes here and there. What kinds of mistakes does this non-native speaker make, and how does he or she distort the precise meanings that we as native speakers can convey?

Lecture Two
When Language Began

Scope: Noam Chomsky has argued that the ability to use language is innately specified in the human brain. The evidence for this includes how quickly we acquire language; how its acquisition seems to be keyed to youth, as are many critical human activities; that actual speech is full of errors and hesitations, yet all humans learn how to speak effectively; and that there are genetic defects that correlate with speech deficits. This view is controversial, however, with many linguists and psychologists seeing language as one facet of cognition rather than as a separate ability.

Outline

I. The Chomskyan hypothesis: Noam Chomsky at the Massachusetts Institute of Technology has argued since the late 1950s that there is evidence that language is a genetic specification located in the human brain. Chomsky argues that humans are programmed very specifically for language, down to a level of detail that includes a distinction between parts of speech, the ways that parts of speech relate to one another, and even parts of grammar as specific as the reason we can say both "You did what?" and "What did you do?" In the last example, the *what* is placed at the front of the sentence, but note that while we can say, "Who do you think will say what?" we cannot then put the *what* at the front and say, "What who do you think will say?" The work of Chomsky and his many followers proposes that things like this are due to certain rules that we are born predisposed to learn.

> You did what?
> What did you do?
>
> Who do you think will say what?
> What who do you think will say? (this sentence is impossible)

II. Arguments for the Chomskyan thesis.

   A. *Speed of acquisition.* All mentally healthy children learn to speak the language that they are exposed to within the first few years of life. We are all familiar with how difficult it is to learn foreign languages as an adult or even as a teenager, yet children acquire those same languages flawlessly with no conscious effort. We do not work to learn our first languages—it "just happens"—despite how very complex languages are. This suggests that we are programmed for the task.

B. *All humans learn to speak.* In contrast to singing or athletic ability, all humans acquire the ability to speak fluently. This includes a great many who are mentally deficient in other ways. This suggests that there is a specific hardwiring for language that overrides culture or individual abilities, as for example, walking.

C. *The critical-age hypothesis.* Language learning ability erodes as we get older.

   1. *Age gradation.* Small children of immigrants learn the new country's language perfectly; people who come to a new country in their early teens often master the language almost perfectly but have slight accents; people who immigrate as full adults often never fully master the new language even with considerable effort.

   2. *Maturational stages in nature.* This parallels a common tendency in organisms for certain genetically specified features to be programmed to appear at certain stages in the life cycle, then erode as they are no longer necessary. Just as ducklings are programmed to fixate on a large moving object as their "mother" and caterpillars are programmed to become butterflies at a certain point, we may be programmed to learn languages early. Our lesser ability later in life would trace to the fact that there is no reason connected to survival for us to be programmed to learn languages later.

   3. *The case of Genie.* A girl named Genie was kept in isolation from human contact from the time she was a toddler until the age of 13 and beaten if she tried to talk. After her release, she never learned to speak fluently, producing such sentences as *I like elephant eat peanut*.

D. *Poverty of the stimulus.* Humans learn language without being taught, and despite the fact that the language they hear is fragmentary and full of false starts. Language as it is actually spoken is rarely as carefully planned out as it is in the artificial medium of writing. Here is a transcription of college students speaking:

A: Yeah. It doesn't help the tree but it protects, keeps the moisture in. Uh huh. Because then it just soaks up moisture. It works by the water molecules adhere to the carbon moleh, molecules that are in the ashes. It holds it on. And the plant takes it away from there.

B: You know, you said how silly it was about my, uh, well, it's not a theory at all. That the more pregnant you are and you see spots before your eyes it's proven that it's the retention of the water.

(Carterette, Edward C., and Margaret Hubbard Jones. *Informal Speech*. Berkeley: University of California Press, 1974, p. 390.)

E. *Specificity of language deficits.* Damage to the brain produces language deficits in specific ways that seem to correspond to two very specific areas of the brain where the ability to speak seems to be located.

1. *Broca's area* appears to control grammar; one person with damage to this area spoke like this:

   Yes…ah…Monday…ah…Dad and Peter Hogan, and Dad…ah…hospital…and ah…Wednesday…Wednesday nine o'clock and ah Thursday…ten o'clock ah doctors…two…two…an doctors and…ah…teeth…yah…

2. *Wernicke's area* appears to control meaning and comprehension; one person with damage to this area spoke like this:

   Oh sure. Go ahead, any old think you want. If I could I would. Oh. I'm taking the word the wrong way to say, all of the barbers here whenever they stop you it's going around and around, if you know what I mean, that is tying and tying for repucer, repucuration, well, we were trying the best that we could…

3. Myrna Gopnik, a linguist at McGill University, and several geneticists have studied a multigenerational family in England in which many people speak rather slowly and often make the kinds of mistakes one would expect of a foreigner, such as *The man fall off the tree* and *The boys eat four cookie*. Their condition is termed *specific language impairment*. Presented with a drawing of a bird-like creature, told that it is called a

wug, shown a picture of two of the creatures, and asked, "Now there are two of them; there are two…?," the impaired members of the family will either wave away the question or answer along the lines of *wugness*.

    4. The affected members of the family have been shown to have a defect in the gene FOXP2.

  F. *Apes versus humans.* It has recently been discovered that chimpanzees and other apes also have the FOXP2 gene but in a slightly different form. This suggests that our version of the gene may give us the ability to use language that apes fall short of.

III. Counterarguments to the Chomskyan thesis.

  A. *Language or cognition?* Many argue that the speed with which humans learn language is but one aspect of the general learning abilities of young people. One might argue that it is remarkable how quickly children learn to pour liquid into a container, throw a ball with aim, or jump rope, and one might observe that the ability to learn such things erodes with age. Few would argue, however, that we are genetically specified for such activities.

  B. *Specific language impairment or mental deficit?* In a subsequent study, the family with language impairment was shown to have a general deficit in intelligence rather than a linguistic deficit specifically, against the hypothesis that there is a discrete genetic endowment for speaking. (Sampson, Geoffrey. *Educating Eve: The "Language Instinct" Debate*. London: Cassell, 1997.)

  C. *How poor is the stimulus?* No one has ever actually documented just how much language children hear is fragmentary, and some researchers suggest that it is much less than Chomsky and his followers assume.

IV. Conclusion.

  A. It seems obvious that humans are programmed to speak on some level. If otherwise, then at least a few groups of humans would be documented who did not speak or did not speak as well as other groups. Furthermore, all babies worldwide would not babble instinctively and eventually learn to speak. After all, no matter how much dogs and cats hear us talk, they do not do so themselves—nor do even the most talented chimpanzees.

B. Just when this ability emerged is currently unknown, but we can be reasonably certain that the humans who migrated out of Africa and populated the world possessed the gift of speech that we are familiar with today.

Essential Reading:

Pinker, Steven. *The Language Instinct*. New York: HarperPerennial, 1994, p. 310.

Sampson, Geoffrey. *Educating Eve: The "Language Instinct" Debate*. London: Cassell, 1997.

Supplementary Reading:

Calvin, William H., and Derek Bickerton. *Lingua ex Machina: Reconciling Darwin with the Human Brain*. Cambridge, MA: MIT Press, 2000.

Deacon, Terrence W. *The Symbolic Species: The Co-Evolution of Language and the Brain*. New York: W.W. Norton, 1997.

Questions to Consider:

1. Linguists who study how children acquire language often note that there is a particular point at which children's ability to speak makes a "quantum leap," such that they are producing full sentences when just a couple of months ago they were limited to two-word utterances, such as "Me eat." Have you noticed such a "quantum leap" in children belonging to you or others?

2. Linguists also note that children learn language to an extent that far surpasses what we "teach" them explicitly. To what extent do you sense that you directly taught your child how to speak—or how not to speak?

Lecture Three
How Language Changes—Sound Change

Scope: A human language is always changing slowly into another one. This is partly because it is natural for sounds to morph into different ones over time. Sounds often change to become more akin to ones before or after them. Sounds at the ends of words tend to wear away. Vowels shift around in the mouth. In English, the last two processes are why *made* is pronounced as it is: the *e* dropped off and an "ah" sound changed to an "ay" sound. Sound change also creates languages where a syllable's tone determines its meaning, as in Chinese.

Outline

I. *Variety among languages*. The first language has now morphed into 6,000 worldwide. The variety among them is awesome: they are not just variations on the French, German, and Russian we learn most often in school, nor are such languages as Chinese the limit in terms of the variation.

   A. There are languages with clicks. The clicks change the meaning of words just as vowels and consonants do in English. The clicks are written with symbols that look rather like profanity in comic strips. In Nama, spoken in Namibia, *hara* means "swallow," !*hara* means "to check out," |*hara* means "to dangle," and †*hara* means "to repulse." One click language has 48 different click sounds.

hara	"swallow"
!hara	"to check out"
|hara	"to dangle"
†hara	"to repulse"

   B. There are languages in Australia with just three verbs. In Jingulu, the only verbs are *come*, *go*, and *do*. Beyond this, Jingulu speakers use such expressions as "go a dive" and "do a sleep."

   C. There are languages that pack a whole sentence's worth of meaning into one word. In Yupik Eskimo, to say, "He had not yet said again that he was going to hunt reindeer," one says, *Tuntussuqatarniksaitengqiggtuq*.

Tuntu-	ssur-	qatar-	ni-	ksaite-	ngqiggte-	uq
reindeer	hunt	will	say	not	again	he

II. Language always changes. The pathway from the first language to all of these variations was based on the fact that language always changes over time.

A. Old English is a foreign tongue to us, as we see in the opening of Beowulf:

Hwæt	we	gardena	in gear-dagum	þeod-cyninga	þrym
what	we	spear-Danes'	in yore-days	tribe-kings'	glory

ge-frunon	hu	ða æþelingas	ellen	fremedon.
heard	how	the leaders	courage	accomplished

Yet there was no time when this language suddenly changed to ours—the process was gradual. This has been happening to all languages around the world since language began.

B. The change from Old English to Modern English—or from the first language to Nama or Jingulu or Greenlandic Eskimo—happened as the result of certain kinds of changes universal in how language changes. In this lecture, we will explore one of these processes, how sounds in a language change over time.

III. Typical sound change processes.

A. *Assimilation.* Many of these changes seem to us to be "sloppy" speaking. For example, in early Latin, the word for *impossible* is *inpossibilis*, but in later Latin, the word was *impossibilis*. The *n* changed to an *m* because the *m* sound is closer to a *p* than *n*. This process is called *assimilation*. Over time, laziness created a new word—the one we borrowed from Latin that is so proper to us today!

in-possibilis > im-possibilis

B. *Consonant weakening.* Similarly, over time, consonants tend to weaken and even disappear.

1. In Latin, the word for *ripe* was *maturus*. In Old Spanish, the word was pronounced the way it is written today: *maduro*; the *t* weakened into a *d*, and the *s* at the end vanished. But in

Castillian Spanish today, the word is actually pronounced "mathuro," with the soft kind of *th* in *mother*. In Old French, the word was similar, pronounced "mathur," but since then, the *th* sound has dropped out completely, and the word is just *mûr*.

LATIN	OLD SPANISH	MODERN CASTILLIAN SPANISH
maturus	maduro	"mathuro"

OLD FRENCH	MODERN FRENCH
"mathur"	mûr

maturus > *mûr* (And this change happened without a break!)

2. This is not "exotic"; it is typical of English, as well. Notice that in the word *bottle*, we do not say "BAH-tull"—we say something like "bahddle." This is because the *t* has weakened to a *d*-like sound over time.

C. *Vowel weakening.* Vowels are fragile as well. The reason *name* is spelled with an *e* at the end is because the spelling corresponds to an earlier stage in our language. Once, the word was "NAH-meh." Over time, the *e* weakened to an "uh" sound: "NAH-muh." Finally, the *e* withered away completely.

D. *Sound shift.* A question here might be why languages do not simply wear away into dust if this is all that sound change is about. In fact, sounds often just transform into new ones.

The Great Vowel Shift. For example, I oversimplified in describing the evolution of the word *name*. The first vowel changed as well: we do not say "nahm" but "naym."

1. *Vowels in the mouth.* This is because starting in the late 1300s, many English vowels began to shift to new ones. Much of our spelling reflects the stage before this shift. To understand it, we need to see how sounds fit into the human mouth. These are the basic vowels the way we learn them in, for example, Spanish:

    i   u

    e   o

        a

2. *How the Great Vowel Shift happened.* Vowels began shifting upwards on this grid.

   Notice that a word such as FOOD is spelled with two o's. It used to be pronounced "fode," but its pronunciation moved up into the "u" region and became what it is now. The spelling has stayed the same, but the language has moved on. Over on the other side of the chart, a word like FEED was originally pronounced "fade," but the sound moved upward so that now it is pronounced with the "i" sound.

   While words such as FEED left their "slots," words with the *ah* sound of "NAH-muh" moved up and took their place. This is why the word is now pronounced "naym"—and why *made* is pronounced the way it is instead of the way it is spelled, "MAH-duh," and so on.

3. *The process continues.* Many Americans today pronounce what is written as *aw* as *ah*, as in "rah fish" instead of "raw fish."

4. *Similar shifts elsewhere.* When the erosion of consonants and the shifting of vowels combine, words can transform so far that we would never perceive any relationship between stage one and stage two without documents showing us the shift through the ages. In Latin, water was *aqua*. In Spanish, the consonant softens to a *g*: *agua*. But in French, the consonant has vanished, and the vowels have changed and combined into one, so that the word is *eau*, pronounced just "oh."

IV. *How languages develop tones.* There are also languages where the pitch at which one utters a syllable determines the very meaning of the word. This is by no means rare; it is typical in East and Southeast Asia and much of Africa. This is another phenomenon created by sound change.

   A. *How tones work.* In Mandarin Chinese, the word *ma* means different things depending on its tone.

má	"hemp"
mà	"scold"
mă	"horse"
mā	"mother"

Mandarin has four tones; Cantonese Chinese has six, so that *fan* can mean "share," "powder," "advise," "divide," "excited," or "grave."

B. *How tones emerge.* This happens as sounds wear away.
1. Suppose there are three words in a language, *pa*, *pak*, and *pas*. Now, when you say *pak*, your voice tends to go up a bit, whereas when you say *pas*, it tends to go down a bit.

Year 1		Last Week
pā	→	pā
pák	→	pá
pàs	→	pà

2. Normally, one wouldn't notice this. But suppose in this language, consonants at the end of words started wearing away, just as the *s* at the end of Latin's *maturus* did to create Spanish's *maduro*. If this happened, then the only way to tell the words apart would be the pitch differences. This is how tone develops in languages.
3. Such pronunciations as "rah fish," then, are symptoms of a general process that helped to transform the first language into the 6,000 new ones that exist today.

Essential Reading:

Bryson, Bill. *The Mother Tongue: English and How It Got That Way*. New York: William Morrow and Co., 1990.

Burgess, Anthony. *A Mouthful of Air: Language, Languages...Especially English*. New York: William Morrow and Co., 1992.

Crystal, David, 1995. *The Cambridge Encyclopedia of the English Language*. Cambridge: Cambridge University Press, 1995 (chapters 3–4: "Old English," "Middle English").

Questions to Consider:

1. To understand how sound change has turned one language into 6,000, think about how you probably say "suh-PRIZE" for *surprise* rather than "ser-PRIZE," or "VEJ-ta-bull" for *vegetable* instead of "VEJ-ah-tah-bull." Are you "wrong" in saying the words this way or just a normal human being?

2. Think of the word *cotton*. Time was that most English speakers pronounced it "KAH-tunn," the way it is spelled. But often, *t's* in the middle of a word can change to a *glottal stop*—that sound in the throat before the vowels in *uh-oh*. The glottal stop is a real "sound" just like *t*—we just don't write it, although it is written in hundreds of other languages. Do you say "KAH-n," with a glottal stop in the middle, or "KAH-tunn"?

Lecture Four
How Language Changes—Building New Material

Scope: Language change is not only sound erosion and morphing but also the building of new words and constructions. This often happens through grammaticalization, where a word that begins as a concrete one (*dog*, *eat*, *red*) becomes one that serves the grammar, placing sentences in time (*soon*), specifying objects (*the*), and so on. The French negative marker *pas* began as the concrete word for *step*. The conjugational endings in Romance languages (Spanish *hablo*, *hablas*, *habla*) began as separate words. Languages also build new words from combining or refashioning old ones.

Outline

I. Even if sounds not only wear away but change, if even the ones that are changing can get worn away too, then why doesn't a language just collapse into dust after a while? The answer is that at all times, a language is developing new material at the same time that it is losing it.

II. Grammaticalization.
   A. Words can be divided into two classes.
   1. *Concrete* words refer to objects, actions, concepts, or traits that any of these have. In other words, nouns, verbs, adjectives, adverbs: *man*, *happiness*, *run*, *overrate*, *red*, *distraught*, *quickly*, *soon*.
   2. *Grammatical* words are those that relate concrete terms to one another or situate a statement in time, space, and attitude. In other words, prepositions, articles, conjunctions, interjections, auxiliaries: *in*, *under*, *the*, *but*, *except*, *hey!*, *so…*, *would*, *not*.

   B. A fundamental process in what happens to a language over time is that grammatical words develop gradually from words that begin as concrete.

   C. The negative marker *pas* in French.
   1. In early French, the regular way to negate a sentence was to put *ne* before it. One did not need to add *pas* afterwards as in Modern French. At this stage in French, *pas* still had a

concrete meaning, *step*, and to add *pas* meant just a stronger version of the negative.

pas "step"	*il ne marche*	"he doesn't walk"
	vs.	
il ne marche pas	"he doesn't walk a step"	

2. At the time, this was part of a general pattern. To make a stronger negation, one added various words to a sentence with *ne*, depending on what kind of action was involved.

pas "step"	*il ne marche*	"he doesn't walk"
	vs.	
il ne marche pas	"he doesn't walk a step"	
mie "crumb"	*il ne mange*	"he doesn't eat"
	vs.	
il ne mange mie	"he doesn't eat a crumb"	
goutte "drop"	*il ne boit*	"he doesn't drink"
	vs.	
il ne boit goutte	"he doesn't drink a drop"	

3. In general in language, an expression that begins as a colorful one either disappears (*peachy keen!*) or dilutes into normality and needs replacing by a new "colorful" expression. In the 1960s and 1970s, for example, to call something or someone *lame* was pretty trenchant; today, it has diluted into meaning roughly "not especially good" and has been replaced by other expressions among the young, such as *from hell*.

4. In French, the "crumb" and "drop" expressions fell away after a while, but the "pas" one held on—although it began fading in power. After a while, there was no real difference between an expression with *pas* and one without one:

il ne marche
    "he doesn't walk"

il ne marche pas

5. In this situation, *pas* no longer seemed to mean *step* at all. By the 1500s, *pas* started to seem as if it were a new way of saying *not*, along with *ne*. And, eventually, it was. This meant that you could use it with any verb, even ones that had nothing to do with walking.

il ne marche pas he not walk **step**	→	il ne marche pas he not walk **not**
il ne mange **pas**		"he doesn't eat"
il ne boit **pas**		"he doesn't drink"

6. Therefore, a word that began as a concrete word for *step* became a piece of grammar, a word to make a sentence negative. This process is called *grammaticalization*.

7. The process has gone even further in colloquial French, where speakers tend to drop the *ne*, leaving *pas* as the only negator word. The change in *pas* from "thing" to "grammar" is now complete!

Standard French:	*il ne marche pas*	"he doesn't walk"
Colloquial French:	*il marche pas*	"he doesn't walk"

8. Recall that this is a worldwide process, not just something that happens in Europe, or to written languages, or to languages spoken by certain people. In the Mandinka language of West Africa, their grammatical word for showing the future, like English's *will*, is *sina*. This word began as two concrete words, *si* and *na*, which mean *sun* and *come*. Together, these words form the word for *tomorrow*: *sina* or "sun come." This word for *tomorrow* was used in expressions with the future so much that it came to be felt as the word for the future itself.

D. Grammaticalization and endings.
   1. To return to the issue of how language rebuilds itself: grammaticalization creates not only new words, such as *pas*, but new endings to replace the ones that sound erosion wears away.

2. For example, in Latin, there were endings expressing the future.

LATIN
amabo "I will love"
amabis "You will love"
amabit "He will love"

3. But there was a newer way of expressing the future, using the verb *habēre* "to have."

LATIN
amabo or *amare habeo* "I will love"
amabis or *amare habes* "You will love"
amabit or *amare habet* "He will love"

4. Over time, the future endings wore away. But at the same time, the *habēre* forms began wearing down and becoming endings on the verb that came before them. What began as concrete words—forms of "to have"—became bits of grammar, endings. The result was a new set of future endings, such as in Italian.

LATIN   ITALIAN

amare habeo → *amer**ò***   "I will love"
amare habes → *amer**ai***   "You will love"

amare habet → *amer**à***   "He/she will love"

5. Overall, any prefixes or suffixes that you find in a language most likely began as separate words. Languages very often continually create their prefixes and suffixes in this way. For example, this kind of process had created the original future endings in Latin. Latin's ancestor Proto-Indo-European had had an expression with a verb and a following verb "to be." This was what created such Latin words as *amabo*.

PROTO-INDO-EUROPEAN   LATIN
am b^{h}wo   →   *ama**bo***

- E. Grammaticalization and new sounds.
    1. Grammaticalization can go so far that it leaves behind bits of material that we barely even think of as suffixes or affixes at all. Consider, for example, this list of related words:

nip	nibble
drip	dribble
dab	dabble
jig	jiggle
	cackle
	babble

    2. We do not usually even realize these words are related, but the *-le* syllable was once an ending in an earlier stage of Germanic, the family that English belongs to. The ending meant "to do something repeatedly within a short time."
    3. Today, we can't make new words with that ending, and often, the original word without *-le* no longer even exists. The ending is just a fossil, but it began as a separate word, now lost to time.
- F. Grammaticalization and new tones.
    1. Sometimes, grammaticalization can also just leave behind a tone! In many languages in Southeast Asia, there was once a prefix that meant that one caused some action to happen. Here is an example from Lahu, a language spoken in China and various Southeast Asia countries:

Stage One		Stage Two	
câ	"to eat"	*câ*	"to eat"
s-câ	"to make someone eat"	*cā*	"to feed"

    2. The *s-* made speakers pronounce the vowel on a lower pitch. But then, erosion wore away the *s-* and left just the lower pitch behind. Now, the low pitch alone shows that one means that an action was caused—as if just a tone meant "to make."

III. Rebracketing.
- A. New words also emerge when speakers redraw the boundaries between two words or combine two words into a single one.

B. Redrawing the boundaries.
   1. The reason some nicknames begin with a seemingly random *n* traces to when the word for *my* was *mīn*, which would be pronounced *mine* today. One would often affectionately say "Mine Ellen" or "Mine Ed." As *mine* became *my*, people started hearing the *n* in these cases as part of the name; thus, we have such nicknames as *Nelly* and *Ned*.
   2. *Hamburger* began as *Hamburger steak*, referring to the origin of the delicacy in Hamburg, Germany. Over time, people began hearing the *-burger* part as a "word," supposing that the "burger" was made of "ham." Now, *burger* is a word of its own and is used with other words—*fishburger* and so on.
C. *Combining two words into one. Alone* began as the two words *all* and *one*. Pronounced together so often, they combined into today's word. To us, it sounds as if the word combines *lone* with a stray *a-*, along the lines, perhaps, of *abubble*. But the word *lone* only arose after *all* and *one* had combined to become *alone*.

IV. Languages are always developing new material, through processes usually too slow to recognize in a lifetime. Only written documents or careful deduction show us the reality of this. From *step* to *not*, from *sun-come* to *will*, from *all one* to *alone*—these changes are part of the natural pathway of any language over time.

Essential Reading:

Bryson, Bill. *The Mother Tongue: English and How It Got That Way*. New York: William Morrow and Co., 1990.

Supplementary Reading:

Grammaticalization has only been widely recognized as a discrete phenomenon, studied, and discussed by linguists over the past 25 years or so, and no popular source on language discusses it other than my own *The Power of Babel*. However, there is a textbook that, although pitched at linguists, can be processed by laymen, especially those seriously interested in the topic: Hopper, Paul J., and Elizabeth Closs Traugott, eds. *Grammaticalization*. Cambridge: Cambridge University Press, 1993.

Questions to Consider:

1. Think about current expressions among younger people, such as *awesome*—remember when that word really meant what the dictionary says it means, that is, "majestic"? Try to list some other words or expressions that once had a more "pungent" meaning than they do now.

2. Chances are you have no problem using *burger* to refer to a disc-shaped piece of food, now often not even made of meat. If this usage is okay, then does this not give you a more tolerant perspective on how language changes in other ways during our lifetimes?

Lecture Five
How Language Changes—Meaning and Order

Scope: Words' meanings naturally shift in various ways through time, usually not having the same connotation at any given time as they did a thousand years before. The word *silly* began meaning "blessed" and acquired its current meaning in a series of gradual steps of reinterpretation. Words' meanings narrow: *meat* once referred to all food; words' meanings broaden: *bird* once referred only to small birds. Languages' word order also changes over time. All possible orders of subject, verb, and object are attested in the world, and one order can change to another one. In English, the verb used to usually come last.

Outline

I. Semantic change.
   A. On the Jack Benny show in the 1940s, Phil Harris said, "Nobody makes love better than me." Obviously he was not using the expression in the meaning it has today—at the time, *make love* meant to court and kiss. Since then, its meaning has drifted. This is an example of semantic change, and despite how uncomfortable many are to see words' meanings shifting over their lifetimes, this kind of change is a central part of how one language became our 6,000.
   B. *Semantic drift.* Often a word's meaning drifts in various directions over time. The word *silly* began in Old English meaning "blessed." But to be blessed implies innocence, and by the Middle Ages, the word meant "innocent":

   1400: Cely art thou, hooli virgyne marie

   But innocence tends to elicit compassion and, thus, the meaning of the word became "deserving of compassion":

   1470: Sely Scotland, that of helpe has gret neide.

There is a fine line, however, between eliciting compassion and seeming weak; as a result, *silly* meant "weak" by the 1600s:

1633: Thou onely art The mightie God, but I a sillie worm.

From here, it was short step to "simple" or "ignorant," and next came the word as we know it, *silly*!

In the following quote from Shakespeare's *The Two Gentlemen of Verona*, we tend to assume that Valentine is making a crack about women, but when the play was written in 1591, he meant that women deserved compassion and help, just like the "poor passengers" he refers to immediately afterward.

I take your offer and will live with you,
Provided that you do no outrages
On silly women or poor passengers.
(*The Two Gentlemen of Verona*, 1591 [iv, i, 70–2])

C. *Semantic narrowing.* Words often come to have more specific meanings than they start with. *Meat* in Old English referred to all food and only later came to refer to animal flesh. We keep a remnant of the old meaning in *sweetmeat*, which refers to candy and fruit, not flesh.

D. *Semantic broadening.* Words also often come to have more general meaning. In Old English, the word *bird* (*brid* at that point) referred only to young birds. The word for birds in general was *fugol*, just as the same root in German, *Vogel*, is today. But *brid* broadened to refer to all birds over time, while *fugol* narrowed and became today's *fowl*, referring only to game birds.

E. *The bigger picture.* Proto-Indo-European had a word $b^h er$, which meant to carry or to bear children. This one word now permeates English in a wide range of meanings that have changed from its original one.
   1. *Basic changes.* We *bear* a nuisance—because toleration is a kind of "carrying." The $b^h er$ root is also in what one bears, a *burden*. Further, the root has come down to us in a narrowed form, referring to one kind of burden, *birth*.

2. *Changes in combination with other words.* Proto-Indo-European speakers often combined b^her with the word *enk*, which meant "to get to"—to carry something over to something was to bring it, and *bring* is exactly the word that came from this: b^her -*enk* became *bring* over time.
3. *Changes in other languages, and back to us.* Meanwhile, sound change turned b^her into *ferre* in Latin, and English borrowed Latin words with *ferre* in them, all with semantically changed descendants of b^her, such as *transfer*, *prefer*, and back to the birthing realm, *fertile*. Greek inherited b^her as *pherein* and shunted it into such words as *pheromone*—chemicals that the air "carries"—*paraphernalia*, and *amphorae*, because things are carried in bottles.

II. Word order.
   A. In English, word order is subject-verb-object: *The boy kicked the ball*. Linguists call this word order *SVO*.
   B. *Different word orders.* But across the world's languages, we find all of the possible orders. There are actually more languages with SOV order than SVO, such as Turkish.

   Turkish
Hasan	öküzü	aldi.
Hasan	ox	bought
S	O	V

   "Hasan bought the ox."

   There are languages where the verb comes first, such as Welsh.

   Welsh
Gwelodd	Alun	gi.
saw	Alun	dog
V	S	O

   "Alun saw a dog."

   Linguists used to consider it impossible that a language would have the direct reverse of our familiar SVO, but languages like this have been discovered, such as the Hixkaryana language spoken by a small group in South America.

©2004 The Teaching Company.

Hixkaryana
Kanawa	yano	toto.
canoe	took	person
O	V	S

"The man took the canoe."

C. Word order and language change.
  1. These different orders are the product of change over time. We cannot be sure what order the first language had, but most linguists think that the first one was either SVO or SOV. Languages tend to change their word order over time; therefore, the various ones in existence today arose when new languages drifted from the first language's word order.
  2. For example, Old English was basically an SOV language.

Old English
Hwi	wolde	God	swa	lytles	þinges	him	forwyrnan?
why	would	God	so	small	thing	him	deny

"Why would God deny him such a small thing?"

Biblical Hebrew put the verb first, but Modern Hebrew has SVO like Modern English.

  3. In a language such as Warlpiri, for example, there actually is no set word order.

Warlpiri
maliki	KA	*wajilipi-nyi*	**kurdu**	<u>wita-ngku</u>
dog	is	chase	child	small

wajilipi-nyi KA maliki **kurdu** <u>wita-ngku</u>
wajilipi-nyi KA **kurdu** <u>wita-ngku</u> maliki
kurdu <u>wita-ngku</u> KA maliki *wajilipi-nyi*
kurdu *wajilipi-nyi* KA <u>wita-ngku</u> maliki
maliki KA **kurdu** <u>wita-ngku</u> *wajilipi-nyi*

"The small child is chasing the dog."

The first language may have been like Warlpiri in this regard, which would mean that any set word order in a language is a change from how language began.

Essential Reading:

Bryson, Bill. *The Mother Tongue: English and How It Got That Way*. New York: William Morrow and Co., 1990 (semantic change).

Crystal, David, *The Cambridge Encyclopedia of the English Language*. Cambridge: Cambridge University Press, 1995 (chapters 3–4: "Old English," "Middle English").

Watkins, Calvert, ed. *The American Heritage Dictionary of Indo-European Roots*. Boston: Houghton Mifflin, 1985 (semantic change).

Supplementary Reading:

Baker, Mark. *The Atoms of Language*. New York: Basic Books, 2001 (word order and how it changes).

Questions to Consider:

1. Has a Shakespeare performance ever worn you out a tad? If the answer is yes, much of the reason is that the words Shakespeare used have changed semantically to such a degree. In your favorite passage of Shakespeare, attend to the footnoted indications of what seemingly normal words he used meant in his time. What do you think about it?

2. Do you think it would be better if words' meanings stayed the same over time? Why or why not?

Lecture Six
How Language Changes—Many Directions

Scope: The first language has become 6,000 because processes of language change can take place in many directions, explainable rather than predictable. In each offshoot group, the original language will change in different ways, until new languages have emerged. Latin split in this way into the Romance languages, as sound changes, grammaticalizations, and meaning changes proceeded differently in each area the Romans brought Latin. This kind of family tree development is a worldwide phenomenon.

Outline

I. One language becomes several.
   A. We have seen some of the tendencies in how languages change: assimilation, consonant weakening, vowel weakening, and sound shift.
   B. But all of these processes can happen in many different ways, and there is no way of predicting which will occur in a language. For example, the *th* sound in *thing* has changed to a *t* in dialects where the pronunciation is *ting* (*dem tings*), but to *f* in Cockney English (*dem fings*).
   C. Often, many groups of people speaking the same language have migrated to several different locations. Chance has it that different changes occur in each new place, and the result over time is several new languages.

II. From Latin to Romance.
   A. This is what happened to Latin as the Romans spread their language from Italy across Europe. In each region, Latin developed into a new language, and these languages today are the ones we know as the Romance languages. These include French, Spanish, Italian, Portuguese, and Romanian, as well as smaller ones, such as Catalan.
   B. *One word becomes five.* The fate of the Latin word *herba* for "grass" in the five main Romance languages shows how language changes in many ways and creates new languages.

```
                        Latin
                        herba
```

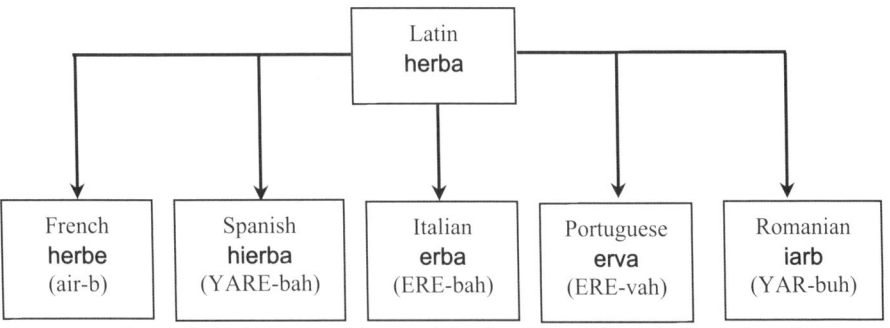

French | Spanish | Italian | Portuguese | Romanian
herbe | hierba | erba | erva | iarb
(air-b) | (YARE-bah) | (ERE-bah) | (ERE-vah) | (YAR-buh)

1. All the languages dropped the *h*—the spellings in French and Spanish maintain it, just as English spelling maintains the "silent" *e*.
2. *Moderate changes.* Italian is one of the closest Romance languages to Latin, and other than the lost *h*, it preserves the word intact. French goes somewhat further and drops the final -*a* as well. Spanish keeps this but changes the *e* to an *ie* (pronounced "yeh"), while Portuguese instead softens the *b* to a *v*.
3. *Radical changes.* Romanian doesn't just insert a *y* sound before the *e* as Spanish does but has a whole new sound *ia* (pronounced "yah"), and the symbol over the final -*a* indicates that this is a new sound, roughly "uh." Consider that similar changes happen to every word in the language, and it is easy to see how one language becomes several new ones.

C. *One sentence becomes five.* Consider a Latin sentence like this one:

Fēminae	id	dedi.
Woman-to	it	I gave

"I gave it to the woman."

Here is this sentence in the five main Romance languages:

French: Je **l'**ai <u>donné</u> à la *femme*.

Latin: *Fēminae* **id** <u>dedi</u>.

Spanish: Se **lo** <u>dí</u> a la *mujer*.
Italian: **L'**ho <u>datto</u> alla *donna*.
Portuguese: **O** <u>dei</u> à *mulher*.
Romanian: Am <u>dat</u>-**o** *femeii*.

The words in italics are for *woman*, the words in bold are for *it*, and the words underlined are for *give*.

1. Word order.
   a. Over time, word order changes, as we can see from the different places that *it* goes in each language.
   b. Latin had flexible word order because of such endings as *-ae* on *fēminae*, which meant "to." The Romance languages have lost most of these kinds of endings on nouns, replacing them with prepositions. This means that word order is not as flexible in Latin's descendants.
2. *Grammar change.* Only the Spanish and Portuguese forms of *give* are descended directly from Latin's *dedi*. The other languages now use a different form of the verb, the participle, used along with a form of the verb *have* (in the construction famous in French as the *passé composé*). This is another way that grammar changes over time—languages develop new ways to express the past, the future, the plural, and so on.
   a. *Word substitution.* In many languages, a Latin word has been replaced by another one—only French and Romanian still use a word derived from *fēmina* to mean "woman" in a neutral sense.
   b. *New words from old ones.* Latin did not have any articles, but all of the Romance languages have them. They developed them by grammaticalization, as Latin words for *that* shortened and changed their meanings from the concrete to the grammatical. But the shape of the articles came out differently in each language: where French has *le*, Spanish has *el*; Italian, *il*; Portuguese, *o*; and Romanian has *-ul*, which it places after the noun instead of before it!

III. From Middle Chinese to seven Chinese languages.
   A. This kind of change has happened to create new languages all over the world. For example, it is often said that there are many Chinese "dialects," as if Mandarin and Cantonese were as similar as American and British English. But actually, these varieties are separate languages, as different from one another as the Romance languages. Only the fact that they are written with the same writing system gives them the appearance of being "the same language."

B. Below is the word for *daughter-in-law* in seven of the Chinese languages. The strange-looking c is pronounced approximately like *ch*. Notice how the consonants and vowels have changed in various directions. Also, the dash and apostrophe symbols over the vowels stand for the tones, and even these have changed in many of the words over time.

	Middle Chinese	
	sjǝk	

Mandarin	Wu (Shanghainese)	Xiang	Gan	Hakka	Cantonese	Min (Taiwanese)
ɕí	sɔ̄ŋ	ɕí	ɕīn	sīm	sām	sīn

(Norman, Jerry. *Chinese*. Cambridge: Cambridge University Press, 1988, p. 198.)

IV. The bigger picture.

  A. It is likely that there was one first language. Even this language immediately started changing. If there had only ever been one human group, then its language would now be completely different from the original one because of the kinds of changes we have seen.

  B. But as soon as human groups started splitting off and migrating to other places—that is, as soon as there was more than group—this meant that the new group or groups' language changed in different ways than the first group's. This meant a new language. Today's 6,000 languages are the product of this process.

Essential Reading:

Note: The following are all readable sources that give "tours" of various languages in the world, highlighting comparisons of family members, including the Romance ones. They do not focus on the change processes themselves but usefully highlight the products of those changes.

Bodmer, Frederick. *The Loom of Language*. New York: W.W. Norton, 1944 (paperback edition, 1985).

Burgess, Anthony. *A Mouthful of Air*. New York: William Morrow & Co., 1992.

Pei, Mario. *The Story of Language*. Philadelphia: J.B. Lippincott, 1949.

Questions to Consider:

1. Do you know anyone who grew up with a language other than English who says that his or her language is "like" another one but hard to understand? Ask this person for a list of 10 words in his or her native language and the other one and examine how the words in the two languages are alike but different—often because of the sound changes we saw in Lecture Three. This will be especially useful with Chinese speakers; for example, ask a Cantonese speaker for Mandarin equivalents of Cantonese words.
2. Have you had experience with both French and Spanish or French and another Romance language? Look at words in both languages and try to figure out what sound change tendencies were local to each.

Lecture Seven
How Language Changes—Modern English

Scope: It is useful to see how language change has happened in our own language even in times relatively close to our own. As recently as Shakespeare, words had meanings more different than is always obvious to us, which interferes with our comprehension of his language. Even in the 1800s, Jane Austen's work is full of sentences that would be considered errors today, and we would be shocked by what was considered acceptable pronunciation of many words in that time. This also shows that language change is less decay than mere transformation, given that we tend to gain alongside the losses.

Outline

I. Language change: Right in our own backyard.
  A. It is plain that language change turned Old English into Modern English. But because Old English and Middle English are so far from us in time, there is a temptation to tacitly sense language change as an "exotic" phenomenon, more typical of the past than our present-day lives.
  B. One way to see that language change is a living reality—in fact, the very nature of speaking—is to look at changes in English more recent than this. English has changed a great deal even in the period when we recognize it as the language we speak.

II. Semantic change.
  A. Along the lines of *silly*'s drift from meaning "blessed" to meaning "foolish," a great many words that Shakespeare used had different meanings for him than they do for us. Most of us do not comprehend Shakespeare as precisely as we often reasonably suppose.
    1. Juliet in *Romeo and Juliet* is often depicted saying, "Wherefore art thou, Romeo?" (ii, ii, 33) with a gesture of looking for her lover. But Romeo is standing right below her during this scene. *Wherefore* actually meant "why." She follows with "Deny thy father and refuse thy name;/Or, if thou

©2004 The Teaching Company. 37

wilt not, be but sworn my love,/And I'll no longer be a Capulet."

   2. Viola tells us in *Twelfth Night* (iii, i, 67–70):

   This fellow is wise enough to play the fool;
   And to do that well craves a kind of wit.
   He must observe their mood on whom he jests,
   The quality of persons, and the time…

   Certainly, she doesn't mean that playing the fool requires being funny. *Wit* did not yet mean "clever humor" in Shakespeare's time: it meant *knowledge*. This usage is now relegated to the margins in English, as in such expressions as *mother wit* or *keep your wits about you*.

   B. When Polonius in *Hamlet* (i, iii, 69) advises Laertes to "Take each man's censure, but reserve thy judgment," we can only assume that he means that Laertes should receive people's criticisms without objecting. But in Shakespeare's time, there was an expression "to take a person's censure," which meant "to size someone up."

III. Change in grammar and pronunciation.

   A. Even as late as Jane Austen's novels in the early 1800s, there are usages that we would consider "mistakes" that were quite proper in Austen's time, such as:

   So, you are come at last
   …and much was ate
   It would quite shock you…would not it?
   She was small of her age

   B. William Cobbett wrote a *Grammar of the English Language in a Series of Letters* to his 14-year-old son. Cobbett's conception of proper English to pass on to his son included such usages as *I bended*, *I sunk*, *loaden*, *shotten*, and *spitten*!

   C. As late as the late 1800s, it was typical in English to say *A house is currently building on Mott Street*, rather than *A house is currently being built*, which was processed as somewhat vulgar.

   D. Long after the Great Vowel Shift that we saw in Lecture Three, pronunciation of English words continued to drift, creating pronunciations different from ours in more ways than just the

English accent we tend to imagine English spoken in before, roughly, the Andrew Jackson presidency. In John Walker's *Pronouncing Dictionary of English* in 1774, Walker recommends that *dismay* be pronounced "diz-may" and *dismiss* "diz-miss" and that *cement* be pronounced "SEE-ment" and *balcony* "bal-COH-nee."

IV. Language change: Decay or growth?

   A. *Language "going to the dogs."* In Modern English, ever fewer speakers are distinguishing *lie* (as in *The pencil is lying on the table*) from *lay* (as in *I laid the pencil on the table*). Similarly, few speakers spontaneously distinguish between *disinterested* (unbiased) and *uninterested* (finding nothing of interest in). Many bemoan this as evidence of decay. But just this kind of decay explains much of how Old English became even the most standardized, formal Modern English.

   B. *Losses of yore.* For example, English once distinguished *here* from *hither*, *there* from *thither*, and *where* from *whither*. Now, these words are strictly archaic. German and related languages still use equivalent words—in German, *ich bin hier* (*I am here*) but I ask you *Komm her*. We can imagine that while these words were being lost in English, some may have complained that a "useful" distinction was being lost, but few of us consider the absence of those words a problem today.

   C. *Ring in the new?* In fact, sometimes, when some English speakers attempt to "compensate" for such losses later on, we process the compensation as "wrong." For example, *you* once was used only in the plural, and *thou* was used for one person. *You* was, specifically, the object form, and *ye* was the subject form. *Thou lookest, ye look*; *I see thee, I see you*. But today, we see such expressions as *you all* and *you'uns* as "wrong"! This shows that it is less loss that disturbs us than change itself.

   D. *The grass is always greener.* The truth is that English has gained features all its own while losing other things, but this is clear only if we compare our language to its relatives, whereas losses are obvious even if we have no familiarity with other languages.

      1. For instance, in Shakespeare's time, while *hither* and *thou* were on their way out of the language, the use of *-ing* in the progressive was emerging. Before this, one said *Right now, I*

sit in the chair—just the way most foreign languages we learn would—where we would now say *Right now, I am sitting in the chair* or *Right now, I am building a house*.
2. In this, English now has a feature that German and its sisters lack. Now, *I sit in the chair* usually means that one sits on a regular basis, while *I am sitting in the chair* means that one is doing it right now. Other Germanic languages—as well as Romance ones—do not make this distinction as clearly or as regularly as English does.

Essential Reading:

Bailey, Richard. *Nineteenth Century English*. Ann Arbor: University of Michigan Press, 1996.

Crystal, David. *The Cambridge Encyclopedia of the English Language*. Cambridge: Cambridge University Press, 1995 (especially chapter 5: "Early Modern English").

McWhorter, John. *Word on the Street: Debunking the Myth of a "Pure" Standard English*. New York: Perseus, 1998 (chapter 4: "The Shakespearean Tragedy").

Questions to Consider:

1. Do you wish that we still said *Come hither* to our children? Why or why not?
2. Collate some examples from your favorite 19th-century novel of usages of English that would be a bit odd today. Do they seem simply "quaint" or like earlier stages of our language, and can you pin down the difference between the two?

Lecture Eight
Language Families—Indo-European

Scope: The Indo-European family is spoken in most of Europe, as well as eastward in Iran and India. The family began in the southern steppes of modern Russia in about 4000 B.C., most likely, and now consists of various subfamilies. Each subfamily teaches lessons about how language changes. For example, in Germanic, bizarre changes in consonants created the difference between such words as *pater*, *père*, and *padre* and our own *father*. Some of the branches have stayed closer to what the Indo-European ancestral language was like, such as the Slavic one containing Russian, while others have morphed so far that they were classified only rather recently as part of the family (Albanian).

Outline

I. The discovery of Indo-European.

 A. In 1786, William Jones, a British jurist and Orientalist, presented an address to the Bengal Asiatic Society in which he observed:

 The Sanskrit language, whatever be its antiquity, is of a wonderful structure; more perfect than the Greek, more copious than the Latin, and more exquisitely refined than either, yet bearing to both of them a stronger affinity, both in the roots of verbs, and in the forms of grammar, than could possibly have been produced by accident; so strong, indeed, that no philologer could examine them all three, without believing them to have sprung from some common source, which, perhaps, no longer exists.

 Jones was making the first official observation of the fact that groups of languages develop from single ones; that is, he inaugurated the study of the natural history of language.

 B. The kind of "affinity" he referred to involved not only word roots in common among Sanskrit, Latin, and Greek but also aspects of grammar. For example, even the case endings on nouns in these languages are clearly related:

tooth in four cases in the languages William Jones referred to:

	SANSKRIT	GREEK	LATIN
nominative	*dán*	*odón*	*dēns*
genitive	*datás*	*odóntos*	*dentis*
dative	*daté*	*odónti*	*dentī*
accusative	*dántam*	*odónta*	*dentem*

C. Jones was referring to ancient languages no longer spoken. But Sanskrit is the ancestor of languages now spoken in India, such as Hindi and Bengali; Latin was the ancestor of the Romance languages; and Ancient Greek has developed into Modern Greek. Linguists later found that the "affinity" Jones referred to applies not only to these languages but to most of the languages of Europe, as well as Iran and India. The "common source" Jones referred to indeed no longer exists, but its descendants are now known as the Indo-European language family.

D. Here is the word for *tooth* in an assortment of these languages:

English	*tooth*
French	*dent*
Italian	*dente*
German	*zahn*
Swedish	*tand*
Russian	*zup*
Polish	*zab*
Welsh	*dant*
Greek	*dhondi*
Albanian	*dami*
Persian	*dandân*
Hindi	*dãt*

II. The emergence of Indo-European.

A. *Location.* Indo-European was by no means the first language or even close. Most evidence suggests that the original Indo-European language was spoken about 6,000 years ago in 4000 B.C., on the steppes of what is now southern Russia. The people are called the Kurgans, referring to burial mounds that they left behind. These people spread westward into Europe and eastward into Iran and India.

B. *Evidence.* We can infer some things about their homeland and culture from what words all or most of the Indo-European languages have in common. Because there are no common words for "palm tree" or "vine," these people were unlikely to be Mediterraneans. Because there is no common word for "oak," they most likely did not emerge in Europe. Because there are common words for "horse," "wheel," and related concepts, we assume that they were using horses as draft animals, and there is archaeological evidence that the Kurgan people had domesticated horses.

C. It has been theorized that Indo-European actually emerged in what is now Turkey, but recent genetic evidence concurs with the traditional southern Russian scenario.

III. Although the Indo-European languages have a great deal in common, they also demonstrate how vastly languages diverge from one another over time.

A. Germanic.

1. This group includes German, Dutch, Swedish and its close relatives Norwegian and Danish, Icelandic, Yiddish, and a few lesser-known languages, such as Frisian and Faroese, as well as Afrikaans spoken in South Africa.

2. A strange sound change took place in the ancestor of this group, explained by Grimm's law, which was named after its discoverer, the same Jacob Grimm who collected folk tales.

Grimm's Law: Latin and Greek to English

pater	**f**ather
podiatrist	**f**oot
tenuous	**th**in
tricolor	**th**ree
decimal	**t**en
dental	**t**ooth

For some reason, in many places where Proto-Indo-European had a *p*, Proto-Germanic switched this to an *f*. This is why Latin has *pater* and Sanskrit has *pitár*, but English has *father* and German has *Vater* (pronounced "FAH-ter"). There were many switches like this; *t* changed to a *th* sound in Germanic, so that while a word we borrowed from Latin, such as *tenuous*, has a *t*, the native Germanic rendition of the word has a *th*. In the same way, Proto-Indo-European's *d* changed into a *t* in Germanic. This is why we have *ten* where Latin had *decem*, the root in some words we borrowed, including *decimal*, and why we have *tooth* where Latin had *dēns*, Sanskrit had *dán*, and Ancient Greek had *odón*.

B. Celtic.
1. These languages are now few, all under severe threat: Irish Gaelic, Scotch Gaelic, Welsh, and Breton spoken in France. Celtic was once spoken across Europe and even in what is now Turkey, but the languages have been edged to the western fringe of Europe by waves of invaders.
2. Celtic languages are well known for their *mutations*, where proper expression requires switching consonants at the beginning of words for no apparent reason, and sometimes the switch alone conveys important meanings.

cath	"cat"
*fy **ngh**ath*	"my cat"
*ei **g**ath*	"his cat"
*ei **ch**ath*	"her cat"

   In Welsh, the word for *cat* is *cath*, but to say *my cat* requires also changing the initial *c* to *ngh*. And then, this kind of change is the only way to distinguish between *his cat* and *her cat*.

C. Baltic versus Italic: Old-fashioned versus up-to-the-minute.
1. Some languages are more conservative than others–that is, they change more slowly. Some Indo-European families have retained a striking amount of Proto-Indo-European structure over the millennia. Others have shed a surprising amount. Lithuanian is of the Baltic family (which today has only one other member, Latvian), and it preserves seven cases, a record among living Indo-European members.
2. As it happens, one of the Indo-European groups most familiar to us is one of the least "faithful" to its ancestor in terms of case endings. Italic once included Latin and other dead languages, but today lives only through the children of Latin alone; Spanish is one. Spanish has not a single one of the Proto-Indo-European case endings. (There is a likely reason for this kind of difference, which we will explore later.)

	LITHUANIAN	SPANISH
tooth	*dantìs*	*diente*
tooth's	*dantiẽs*	*del diente*
to the tooth	*dañčiui*	*al diente*
tooth (accusative)	*dañtį*	*diente*
on the tooth	*dantyjè*	*sobre el diente*
with the tooth	*dantimì*	*con el diente*
Oh, tooth!	*dantiẽ!*	*¡Ay, diente!*

D. Albanian and Armenian: Black sheep.
1. Other groups have been so innovative that they are difficult to even recognize as family members. Albanian is the language that would have been spoken by the *Twelfth Night* characters because the play takes place east of the Adriatic in the Illyrian region. Armenian is spoken between the Black Sea and the Caspian Sea. Both of these languages are the only members of their family.
2. Both have borrowed many words from other language groups: only about 1 in 12 Albanian words is native to the language and only about 1 in 4 Armenian ones. Both languages have also wended quite far along their own paths of development. Albanian wasn't even discovered to be Indo-European until 1854, and Armenian was long thought to be a kind of Persian. Here are the numbers 2 through 9 in Albanian and Armenian, compared to "normal" Indo-European languages. The Albanian and Armenian words come from the same ancestor as the other languages' words do, but look how differently they often come out:

ENGLISH	SPANISH	FRENCH	GERMAN	GREEK	ALBANIAN	ARMENIAN
two	dos	deux	zwei	dúo	dü	erku
three	tres	trois	drei	treîs	tre	erek'
four	cuatro	quatre	vier	téttares	katër	č'ork'
five	cinco	cinq	fünf	pénte	pesë	hing
six	seis	six	sechs	héks	gjashtë	vec'
seven	siete	sept	sieben	heptá	shtatë	evt'n
eight	ocho	huit	acht	októ	tetë	ut'
nine	nueve	neuf	neun	ennéa	nëntë	inn

E. *Indo-European: The "In do" part.* In India, Indo-European languages have taken on many features from the grammars of languages spoken by peoples who first occupied the area, such as the Dravidian languages that are still spoken in southern India today, including Tamil. An example is word order. In Hindi, the verb comes at the end of the sentence, and prepositions come after nouns. Thus, in Hindi, *I met Apu* is "I Apu-with met-did."

Mẽ	Apu	se	mila	tha.
I	Apu	with	meet	did

"I met Apu."

Essential Reading:

Burgess, Anthony. *A Mouthful of Air*. New York: William Morrow & Co., 1992 (chapters 12–16).

Crystal, David. *The Cambridge Encyclopedia of Language*. Cambridge: Cambridge University Press, 1987 ("The Indo-European Family").

Supplementary Reading:

Ramat, Anna Giacalone, and Paolo Ramat, eds. *The Indo-European Languages*. London: Routledge, 1998.

Wells, Spencer. *The Journey of Man: A Genetic Odyssey*. Princeton: Princeton University Press, 2002 (chapter 8: "The Importance of Culture").

Questions to Consider:

1. Ask someone you know who speaks Russian, Polish, Persian, Greek, or another Indo-European language how to say *My father spoke to a woman one day*, write the sentence down, and try to figure out how the words relate to English words with similar meanings. If you do this, you will see the essence of how language changes: this person's language started as the same one that became English!
2. English was once the Proto-Indo-European language. Now it is not, nor is any other language that grew from it. Can we put a value judgment on this? Do we wish that the "Proto-Indo-European heritage" could be preserved?

Lecture Nine
Language Families—Tracing Indo-European

Scope: Linguists have deduced what Proto-Indo-European was like by comparing the modern languages: if more have a *b* in a word than a *v*, it is likely that the original word had a *b*. Along these lines, we can assume that the word for *sister-in-law* was *snusos*, even though in Armenian today, it is simply *nu*! Sometimes, careful guesses have been confirmed by newly discovered ancient documents, some Indo-European subfamilies being known only in this fashion.

Outline

I. Reconstructing the ancestor.

    A. In the previous lecture, I occasionally referred to features that the first Indo-European language had. One might ask, however, just how we can know what that language was like. It was not written: our first written evidence of Indo-European comes after the first language had already split into several new ones, including Sanskrit, Latin, Ancient Greek, and Gothic.

    B. Over the past two centuries, linguists have reconstructed what the first Indo-European language was probably like by deducing from the living languages and the older ones that were written. The hypothetical language is called *Proto-Indo-European*. There is a vast "dictionary" of Proto-Indo-European words, and much is known about its endings and other aspects of its grammar.

II. Reconstructing Proto-Indo-European words.

    A. Here is *sister-in-law* in seven Indo-European languages:

Armenian	*nu*
Sanskrit	*snuṣā́*
Russian	*snokhá*
Old English	*snoru*
Latin	*nurus*
Greek	*nuós*
Albanian	*nuse*

Actually, in Albanian and Armenian, the meaning of the root is now *bride*—semantic change is eternal.

To discover what the Proto-Indo-European word for *sister-in-law* was, we trace backwards. This method is called *comparative reconstruction*.

B. Some of the words begin with *sn-*, while others begin with *n-*. To decide whether the Proto-Indo-European word began with *sn-* or *n-*, we seek an account that squares with typical sound-change processes. Along those lines, it is more likely that several separate languages lost an *s*—by ordinary sound erosion—than that several separate languages somehow developed *s* for some reason (and always *s*). Thus, we know that the word began with *sn-*.

C. To decide whether the first vowel was an *o* or a *u*, we choose *u*, because more of the words have *u* than *o*. Again, it is more likely that a few words changed a *u* to an *o* than that many changed an *o* to a *u*. Thus, the first word would have begun with *snu-*.

D. The second consonant is a little harder to decide on. Three words—half of our set—have an *s*, but this is not a majority. Here, some additional information nudges us in the right direction. In many Latin words, *r* between vowels had begun as *s*. In Russian, many *kh* sounds trace back to *s* in earlier Slavic languages. This gives us a majority for *s*, and we can assume that the first word began with *snus-*.

E. The ending gives us a surprise.
  1. Because *sister-in-law* is a feminine concept, if we are familiar with such languages as Spanish and Italian, in which *-o* is the masculine ending and *-a* the feminine one, we expect the original ending to have been *-a*. But Greek and Latin have *-ós* and *-us*, masculine endings, and in Armenian, when the word is given case endings, an *o* appears on the stem: *nuo*.
  2. This is just three, not a majority. But then logic beckons: given that sisters-in-law are women, why would Sanskrit and Russian speakers have changed a feminine ending to a masculine one? In bizarre cases like this, we suppose that the ending must have originally been masculine and that some languages naturally "fixed" this over time and changed it to the more logical feminine ending. Thus, we have our original

Proto-Indo-European word, the mysteriously cross-gender word *snusos*.

F. Through comparative reconstruction, then, we can know that a word that is merely *nu* in Albanian today began as the longer, chunkier *snusos*. Indo-Europeanists mark these hypothetical forms with an asterisk: **snusos*.

III. *Reconstructing Proto-Indo-European sounds.* One way we know this method is valid is that sometimes, unexpected discoveries confirm what began as surmises.

A. Languages have preferences in terms of how syllables are built. In Japanese, the only consonant that can occur at the end of a word is *n*. Otherwise, all words end in a vowel—*arigatō*, *sushi*, *kamikaze*, and so on. In Chinese, most words have just one syllable. In Proto-Indo-European, most words reconstructed have one vowel sandwiched between two consonants, such as the *b^her-*, "to bear" root we saw in Lecture Five, or **med-*, "to measure."

b^her- "to bear"
**med-*   "to measure"

B. But then there are Proto-Indo-European roots where instead of a final consonant, there is a first consonant, then a long vowel. A long vowel is marked with a macron: **dō-* "to give," **pā-* "to protect."

**dō-* "to give"
**pā-* "to protect"

C. In the late 1800s, pioneering linguist Ferdinand de Saussure proposed that these words used to follow the normal consonant-vowel-consonant pattern, but that the vowels were now, as it were, stretching into a spot where there had once been a consonant.

1	2	3
b^h	e	r
m	e	d
d	o	o
p	a	a

Saussure assumed that the consonants must have been breathy ones pronounced back in the throat (such as *h*), given that sounds like this often make a vowel before them longer in languages around the world.

STAGE ONE

1	2	3
b^h	e	r
m	e	d
d	o	H
p	a	H

STAGE TWO

1	2	3
b^h	e	r
m	e	d
d	o	o
p	a	a

D. De Saussure's theory was rejected because there was no concrete evidence that these sounds had existed. But early in the 20th century, ancient tablets written in cuneiform script were found in Turkey, dating as far back as the 1700s B.C. Many of them were written in what turned out to be an extinct Indo-European language, now called Hittite. Hittite has a consonant sound, written as an *h*, in some of the places where de Saussure guessed it would be.

E. Thus, today, Proto-Indo-European is assumed to have had these sounds, called *laryngeals*, although no living language preserves them.

IV. *Filling out the genealogy.* Hittite was one of several languages now known only from documents found in Turkey, constituting a whole extinct Indo-European family called Anatolian. Another extinct family was discovered in the 20th century.

A. At the end of the 1800s, Buddhist manuscripts were discovered in western China, dating as far back as 600 A.D., in an unknown language. Luckily, the script was related to the one now used for Hindi, and the manuscripts were well-known Buddhist texts. The language turned out to be an Indo-European one—it had words like *noktim* for night—but its name and speakers were a mystery.

B. But one of the documents was written instead in the Uighur language, related to Turkish, and said that it was translated from a language called "twghry." As it happens, Greek historians mention a people who migrated from the Fergana Valley (at the intersection of what is today Uzbekistan, Tajikistan, and Kyrgyzstan) to northern India and converted to Buddhism. The Greeks call them the Tokharoi—note the match to "twghry" in the consonants.

C. Various clues allowed a match between the people the Greeks mentioned and the manuscripts. Frescoes painted by Buddhists in western China around 900 A.D. depict Caucasian people. Mummies have been found in the area with ample facial hair, light eyes, and high, bridged noses; these mummies are also very tall. Further, contemporary Chinese accounts mention white people in the area.

D. Thus, Tocharian was a lost branch of Indo-European, spoken by white peoples who migrated into China.

Essential Reading:

Dalby, Andrew. *Dictionary of Languages*. New York: Columbia University Press, 1998 (entries on Indo-European and its various branches).

Watkins, Calvert, ed. *The American Heritage Dictionary of Indo-European Roots*. Boston: Houghton Mifflin, 1985, pp. xiii–xiv.

Supplementary Reading:

Arlotto, Anthony. *Introduction to Historical Linguistics*. Boston: University Press of America, 1972.

Barber, Elizabeth Wayland. *The Mummies of Ürümchi*. New York: W.W. Norton & Co., 1999.

Questions to Consider:

1. If we could reconstruct the very first language through the above methods, what purpose or benefit might this serve? This is not a trick question: just explore.

2. You may have noticed that there are many similarities between how languages evolve and how animals and plants do. However, there are also differences between natural selection and language evolution—which ones come to mind?

Lecture Ten
Language Families—Diversity of Structures

Scope: This lecture shows how language change in different directions can produce two language families extremely different from Indo-European and from one another. Semitic includes Arabic and Hebrew and assigns basic meanings to three-consonant sequences and creates words by altering the vowels around them: in Hebrew, *katav* is "he wrote," *kotev* is "he writes," and *ktiv* is "spelling." In Sino-Tibetan languages, such as Chinese, a sentence tends to leave more to context than we often imagine possible, and a series of particles at the end of a sentence conveys shades of attitude that we barely think of as "grammar" at all.

This lecture introduces two language families that demonstrate how different the product of language change over time can be.

Outline

I. Semitic.

  A. The best-known Semitic languages are Arabic and Hebrew, spoken in the Middle East, along with a few others, such as Aramaic (the language of Jesus). There are records of many extinct Semitic languages, such as Akkadian (written in cuneiform) and Phoenician.

  B. Semitic languages are almost unique in the world in basing words on roots of three consonants, creating a range of related meanings by altering the vowels around and between them and adding prefixes and suffixes.

  C. For example, in Arabic, the root K-T-B has to do with the concept of writing. Here is the way the language creates a wide range of meanings from this one root:

ka**t**a**b**a	"he wrote"	ki**t**ā**b**	"book"
ya**kt**u**b**u	"he writes"	**k**u**t**u**b**ī	"bookseller"
ka**tt**a**b**a	"to make write"	ma**kt**a**b**	"office"
ʻa**kt**a**b**a	"to dictate"	ma**kt**u**b**	"letter"

kātaba	"to correspond"	mukātaba	"correspondence"
'inkataba	"to subscribe"	kātib	"writer"
'iktataba	"to copy"	kitba	"writing"

The dash over the vowel means that the vowel is long; notice that the difference in vowel length can make a difference in meaning. The apostrophe stands for a glottal stop, as in the first sound one makes in saying "uh-oh."

D. Language families can spread across very different cultures and peoples. Most Semitic languages are actually spoken in Ethiopia, across the Red Sea from the Middle East. This is why, for example, "night" is *laila* in Hebrew and *leylat* in Amharic, the major Ethiopian Semitic language.

E. The sentence "You're wearing it" looks quite different in Hebrew and Amharic. But if we look closely, we can see a similar trio of consonants, the Semitic root for wearing clothes. Hebrew has L-V-SH, and lurking in the Amharic word is the similar L-B-S.

"You're wearing it."

HEBREW			AMHARIC
ata	loveš	oto	tilebsewalleh
you	wear	it

II. East and Southeast Asia.

A. This area actually contains several families. The main three are *Sino-Tibetan*, which includes Chinese, Tibetan, and Burmese; *Tai-Kadai*, which includes Thai and Laotian; and *Austroasiatic*, which includes Vietnamese and Khmer.

B. *Heavy reliance on context.* These languages stand out in being especially telegraphic compared to most languages. It is natural to suppose that a "normal" language has separate words for *he* and *she*, or words for *a* and *the*, or must always express pronominal concepts, such as "I" and "you," either with a word or with the endings that we learn in Spanish. But Cantonese goes against all of these notions, as do most languages in this area. Notice also how differently Cantonese puts a thought together than English does.

Kéuih ngóh tùhnghohk lèihga.
he/she my classmate you-know
"He's my classmate."

Yuhng hùhng bāt sé hóu dī
use red pen write good a-bit
"It's better to write with a red pen."

C. *Particles.* Thus, an English speaker thinks of *a* and *the* and *he* and *she* as crucial things to mark in a language. But there are things that an English speaker would *not* conceive of as "grammar" that speakers of these languages do. For example, where we would say "This machine's very reliable" in a tone of voice objecting to someone denying this, in Cantonese the assertive attitude that this tone of voice conveys is also marked with a particle at the end of the sentence:

Nī bouh gēi hóu hókaau **ge**.
this machine very reliable
"This machine's very reliable."

In the same way, if someone asked us why we weren't sleeping and we answered "It's too noisy," we leave it to context that we are saying this in response to a situation going on at that time. But in Cantonese, this is actually "said," with a particle that conveys immediate relevance:

Taai chòuh **la**.
too noisy
"It's too noisy!" (I can't sleep.)

You can even combine particles like this. In this sentence, the person is both asserting and speaking of something immediately relevant; therefore, *ge* and *la* are used together.

Ngóh yiu Vincent deui ngóh hóu jauh dāk **ge la**.
I want Vincent to me good then okay
"All I want is for Vincent to be good to me."

Cantonese has about 30 particles like this, marking attitudes that English often leaves to context or conveys with intonation. There were particles in the first Cantonese examples we saw in section II.B. of this lecture.

D. *Classifiers.* Instead of marking nouns with articles as in English, languages in this area use classifiers with nouns according to their shape, especially with numbers. This practice is similar to using such English expressions as *two head of cattle*, but these languages use this kind of construction regularly.

yāt jēung tói	"one table"
yāt jēung jí	"sheet of paper"
yāt jek gāidáan	"one egg"
yāt jek sáubīu	"one wristwatch"
yāt jī bāt	"one pen"
yāt jī dék	"one flute"
yāt tìuh louh	"one road"
yāt tìuh sèh	"one snake"

Cantonese uses *jēung* with flat objects, such as tables and paper; *jek* with round objects; *jī* with cylindrical objects; *tiuh* with long, thin objects; and so on. There are dozens of these words.

Essential Reading:

Comrie, Bernard, Stephen Matthews, and Maria Polinsky, eds. *The Atlas of Languages*. New York: Facts on File, 1996.

Crystal, David. 1987. *The Cambridge Encyclopedia of Language*. Cambridge: Cambridge University Press, 1987 ("Other Families").

Supplementary Reading:

"Languages of the World." *Encyclopedia Brittanica*. 1998.

Kaye, Alan. "Arabic." *The World's Major Languages*. Edited by Bernard Comrie, 1990, pp. 664–685.

Matthews, Stephen. *Cantonese: A Comprehensive Grammar*. London: Routledge, 1994.

Questions to Consider:

1. Languages differ greatly in what kinds of shadings they choose to mark and how. English uses intonation, where many languages might have

distinct words. For example, if someone says to you *You've ALREADY seen me happy*, the intonation alone implies that you are about to see the person happy again. Think of some other cases where intonation conveys specific meanings and intimations that would be lost on paper.

2. Try writing out some English sentences where no vowel sounds are indicated except "ee" and "oo" (notice that the correspondence between this and particular letters will be rough). This approximates how Arabic and Hebrew are usually written (it is not that vowels are not indicated at all). Is there a significant disadvantage?

Lecture Eleven
Language Families—Clues to the Past

Scope: How language families are distributed gives information about how humans have spread through migration. Generally, where a language family's members are most numerous is where the family emerged, because there has been more time in the original location for the languages to diverge into new ones. This principle shows that the massive Austronesian family, now spread across Southeast Asia's islands out across the South Seas to Polynesia, began on the small island Formosa, where two dozen languages representing three separate subfamilies are spoken. Similar facts shed light on the history of Africa and North America.

Depending on one's metrics for counting them, there are at least dozens and at most hundreds of language families in the world. Their distribution across the planet often gives us clues as to how humans have migrated over time.

Outline

I. Austronesian.
   A. There are almost 1,000 Austronesian languages. They are mostly spoken in the islands of Southeast Asia and eastward of New Guinea and Australia. Most of these languages are relatively similar, even across spaces as vast as that between the Philippines, Malaysia, and the South Seas. Malagasy is an Austronesian language, indicating that people sailed all the way from Southern Asia to Madagascar. The language is still similar to its sisters.

   Cognates in Austronesian languages:

	TAGALOG	MALAY	FIJIAN	SAMOAN	MALAGASY
stone	*bato*	*batu*	*vatu*	*fatu*	*vato*
eye	*mata*	*mata*	*mata*	*mata*	*maso*

   B. The Austronesian languages that are most different from the others are spoken in Taiwan. In fact, Austronesian consists of four subfamilies, and three of them are spoken on this small island.

These three subfamilies consist only of a dozen-odd living languages. But linguists take this kind of contrast in diversity as evidence that the family originated in Taiwan, because where the languages have existed the longest, they would have had the most time to diverge from one another.

C. On the other hand, the Austronesian languages that are most akin to one another are the Polynesian ones.

Cognates in Polynesian languages:

	TONGAN	SAMOAN	TAHITIAN	MAORI	HAWAIIAN
louse	*kutu*	*'utu*	*'utu*	*kutu*	*'uku*
lizard	*moko*	*mo'o*	*mo'o*	*moko*	*mo'o*
to laugh	*kata*	*'ata*	*'ata*	*kata*	*'aka*

This suggests that they are the newest Austronesian languages, because they haven't had time to diverge significantly yet. Archaeology supports this conception of Austronesian's history. Evidence suggests that western Polynesia was settled between 1500 and 1200 B.C., while the islands furthest from the western ones, such as New Zealand and Hawaii, appear to have been settled between 600 and 1000 A.D. Meanwhile, hill people in Taiwan and Polynesians share some cultural traits, such as using bark beaters to make clothes.

II. Bantu.

A. There are about 500 Bantu languages. The best known is Swahili. They are spoken south of the Sahara in Africa. They are generally quite similar to one another, varying about as much as the Romance languages do.

B. Like Taiwan with Austronesian, Cameroon and eastern Nigeria are the exception with Bantu. Here, the languages differ much more from one another. This suggests that the family emerged here, and archaeology shows that the Bantu people began migrating southward from this area around 3000 B.C. This means that most of the languages are so close because they are mostly rather new.

C. There is another clue that Bantu is a new group. In southwestern Africa, there is an area where click languages—called Khoi-San languages by linguists—are spoken rather than Bantu ones.

- **D.** Two click languages are also spoken up in Tanzania. The question is why this group is situated amidst Bantu speakers. It would appear that Khoi-San was once much more widespread and that Bantu speakers overran most of these languages and left behind only small islands. In Bantu-speaking areas, fossil skulls have been found of the Bushman type. Some Bantu languages spoken near Khoi-San ones have some clicks.
- **E.** Thus, the distribution of language families today is quite different from the original one. Basque is a similar case, surrounded by Indo-European languages. The Basques have some distinct genetic markers from other Europeans, and this and other evidence shows that Basque is a remnant of a larger group once spoken across Europe. Indo-European speakers migrated into Europe and largely replaced these earlier languages; Basque is a lone living clue to that past.

III. Native American languages.
- **A.** Before Europeans came to the New World, about 400 separate languages were spoken in North America and about 670 in Central and South America. Most of these languages are now gradually dying out.
- **B.** The distribution of these languages poses a problem. The New World was settled from Asia, across the Bering Strait. We would expect that the highest diversity, then, would be in Alaska and Canada. Instead, the north is covered by just two families, while dozens of others are found further south. Diversity is generally highest in South America, California, and other places.
- **C.** This suggests that something interrupted the linguistic "timeline" in the north; genetic and geographical evidence suggests that the last Ice Age largely drove away people in the north, so that the area was repopulated after the thaw. This means that the languages there have had less rather than more time to diverge from one another. The language distribution alone suggests this, even without the other evidence.

IV. Inferring further back: The first language?
- **A.** The Khoi-San languages, in this light, may shed more light on the human past. There are about 50 of these languages, but they do not form a tidy group as, for example, Indo-European does. There is

barely a typical "Khoi-San" grammar—some bristle with case endings like Latin, while others are more "naked" like Chinese, and there are not many words that appear in similar guises in all or even many of them. This suggests that these languages are quite ancient, having diverged over a vast amount of time. In addition, the two click languages in Tanzania are extremely different from the ones spoken in the south, as well as from one another.

B. In this light, it is important that humans emerged in Africa, that early *Homo sapiens* fossils are smaller than today's humans (Bushmen are rather small people), and that it is very hard to conceive of how clicks could emerge in a language. It may be that the clicks were present in the first language(s) and have disappeared almost everywhere but where they originally existed.

C. Thus, the click languages may be the descendants of the first one.

Essential Reading:

Comrie, Bernard, Stephen Matthews, and Maria Polinsky, eds. *The Atlas of Languages*. New York: Facts on File, 1996.

Dalby, Andrew. *Dictionary of Languages*. New York: Columbia University Press, 1998.

Diamond, Jared. *Guns, Germs, and Steel*. W.W. Norton & Co., 1997 (especially chapter 17: "Speedboat to Polynesia" and chapter 19: "How Africa Became Black").

Supplementary Reading:

"Languages of the World." *Encyclopedia Brittanica*. 1998.

Finegan, Edward. *Language: Its Structure and Use*. Fort Worth, TX: Harcourt Brace, 1989.

Oppenheimer, Stephen. *The Real Eve: Modern Man's Journey out of Africa*. New York: Carroll & Graf, 2003 (chapter 7: "The Peopling of the Americas").

Questions to Consider:

1. Two language families share India: the Indo-Aryan group, including Hindi, Punjabi, and Bengali, and the Dravidian group, including Tamil and Kannada. Most of the Dravidian languages are spoken on the

southern "tip" of the country, but a few are scattered further north. What does this suggest about ancient population movements in India?

2. It is highly likely that languages related to Basque once coated much of Europe, just as languages now lost were likely spread throughout southeastern Asia before the Chinese moved southward. Language death, then, is a natural process, yet today, many people are dedicated to preserving minority languages in danger of extinction. How do we reconcile these sincere efforts with the realities of the past?

Lecture Twelve
The Case Against the World's First Language

Scope: A few linguists have claimed to reconstruct words from the world's first language, but this work is extremely controversial. For one, language change is so thorough that it is hard to imagine why any words would have stayed identifiable in any language after as long as 150,000 years. Moreover, languages tend to have words in common with similar sounds and meanings just by chance. There are also problems with the "Proto-World" hypothesis in terms of reconstruction of language families' proto-words.

Outline

I. Words from the first language?

    A. Linguists Joseph Greenberg and Merritt Ruhlen have claimed to have reconstructed words from the world's first language, which they call Proto-World. They compared words with similar meanings in hundreds of languages and deduced what the original form would have been.

    B. Although this work has often been covered with interest in the media, most linguists who specialize in language change have vehemently rejected it. It is tempting to suppose that Greenberg and Ruhlen are typical examples of despised renegades who history will eventually prove right. But based on what we have seen so far in this course, we can see that there is a great deal of validity to the objections.

II. First objection: The depth of language change.

    A. The shape of words changes so much over time that the question is why any one of them would stay recognizable in any language after 150,000 years. Recall Proto-Indo-European *snusos* becoming *nu* in Albanian. Languages also substitute new roots for old ones to express meanings: Spanish, Russian, and Greek are all Indo-European but use different roots for bread (*pan, xleb, psomi'*).

B. Algonquian is a family of Native American languages, including Cree and Cheyenne spoken in Montana and Oklahoma. Proto-Algonquian words have been recovered through comparative reconstruction; the word for *winter*, for example, was *peponwi*. But the word in Cheyenne that has developed from this root is *aa'* —because of gradual changes over just 1,500 years.

winter from Proto-Algonquian to Cheyenne:

p	e	p	o	n	w	i
p	e	p	o	n		
	e		o	n		
	a		i	n		
	a		i			
	a		i	'	i	
	a		a	'	i	
	a		**a**	'		

III. Second objection: Comparative reconstruction *über alles*.

A. Language change specialists trace proto-language words by painstaking deduction along the lines that we saw with **snusos*. But writing has existed for only a tiny fraction of the time that language has existed (6,000 years); we have no access to actual data to trace Proto-World words step by step backward. Instead, Greenberg and Ruhlen rely on a broader "eyeballing" technique.

B. Here are various words that lead them to reconstruct **tik* as the first word for "one" or "finger."

Evidence of Proto-World form **tik*, "one, finger":

Latin	*digitus*	"finger"
Old English	*tahe*	"toe"
Dinka (Sudan)	*tok*	"one"
Turkish	*tek*	"only"
Korean	*(t)tayki*	"one, thing"
Japanese	*te*	"hand"
Tibetan	*(g-)tśig*	"one"
Vietnamese	*tay*	"hand"
Southern Tasmanian	*mo-took*	"forefinger"
Eskimo	*tik(-iq)*	"index finger"

Mohawk	*tsi'er*	"finger"
Chibcha (S. America)	*ytiquyn*	"finger"

    C. Ruhlen objects that comparative reconstruction is not a necessary condition for establishing a relationship between languages:

    Were a biologist to demand a complete reconstruction of Proto-Mammal, together with a complete explanation of how this creature evolved into every living mammal, before he would accept the fact that human beings are related to cats and bats, he would not be taken seriously. Yet it is just this kind of linguistic nonsense that has been taught in universities by Indo-Europeanists for so long that most linguists are unaware of its mythological nature. (Ruhlen, Merritt. *The Origin of Language: Tracing the Evolution of the Mother Tongue.* New York: John Wiley & Sons, 1994, p. 133.)

IV. Chance resemblances.

    A. Yet a problem remains: there are many chance resemblances between words with similar meanings in any two languages. Here are examples from English and Japanese, which no linguist considers to be related in any significant way.

JAPANESE	meaning	ENGLISH
mō	more	*more*
sō	like that	*so* (as in *just so*)
sagaru	hang down	*sag*
nai	not	*not*
namae	name	*name*
mono	thing (a single entity)	*mono-* "one"
miru	see	*mirror* (which one sees in)
taberu	eat	*table* (where one eats)
atsui (ott-SOO-ee)	hot	*hot*
hito	man	*he*
yo	emphatic particle	*Yo!*
kuu	"feed your face"	*chew*
inki	dark-spirited, glum	*inky* (dark)
o	honorific prefix	*O* ("O, mighty Isis")

B. A language can have only so many consonants together and so many vowels together: there is a limit on the degree to which syllables in human language can vary. This shows the danger in the "eyeballing" strategy.

V. Comparing proto-language forms.

A. Greenberg and Ruhlen deduce not from hundreds of languages together but from words in the proto-languages that have been deduced, like Proto-Indo-European, for each family. But even here, their conception of "similarity" leads to questions.

B. Here are 12 proto-language forms for *water*. Greenberg and Ruhlen reconstruct from these that the Proto-World form would have been *$aq'wa$.

Evidence for Proto-World *$aq'wa$* for *water* as reconstructed in 12 family proto-languages:

k''ā	nki	engi	ak'^{w}a	rt^s'q'a	nīru
ak^{w}ā	'oχ^{w}a	namaw	okho	gugu	akwā

C. *$ak^wā$, *ak'^wa, and *$'oχ^wa$ are clearly similar, but they are from, respectively, Proto-Indo-European, Afro-Asiatic, and Caucasian. The problem is that these families all arose in regions close to one another— southern Russia, the Middle East, the Caucasus mountains. It is possible that these families share a common ancestor, then— but this is just three out of a great many families in the world. Their ancestor was not the world's *first* language—it would have been one of legions of descendants of that first language.

D. *$akwā$ is only the proto-form for Algonquian, but Greenberg and Ruhlen present it as a proto-form for most of the languages of North America. Beyond Algonquian, in assorted Native American languages, we find forms for *water* (and related meanings) as disparate as *uk, yok-ha, 'aha', ku'u, iagup, uku-mi,* and *oxi'*.

Essential Reading:

Ruhlen, Merritt. *The Origin of Language: Tracing the Evolution of the Mother Tongue.* New York: John Wiley & Sons, 1994, pp. 115–119.

Wright, Robert. "Quest for the Mother Tongue." *Atlantic Monthly* 267 (1991): 39–68.

Supplementary Reading:

Matisoff, James. "On Megalocomparison." *Language* 66 (1990): 106–120.

Questions to Consider:

1. Most historical linguists think that comparative reconstruction will never recover the first Native American language or languages and that this closes the issue. The Proto-World specialists object that there must have been such a language, that we can glean at least some information about it through their more general techniques, and that to neglect to try this is to give up on the larger enterprise of charting the birth and migrations of our species. Whose side would you be on?

2. Based on what we have seen about how language changes, what kind of grammar do you think the first language might have had? Why?

Lecture Thirteen
The Case For the World's First Language

Scope: Most linguists' reception of the Proto-World work has been less skeptical than hostile, and as often in such cases, there is more truth to the theory than many admit. For example, there is increasing evidence that many of the world's families do trace to "mega-ancestors," even if evidence for a Proto-World remains lacking. The Proto-World school's reconstruction of features of the Native American proto-language are promising, and one of these linguists has recently discovered a likely valid link between languages whose speakers have had no contact for 50,000 years.

Outline

I. Smaller superfamilies: Eurasiatic.

  A. Greenberg and Ruhlen follow in a tradition that traces back to the early 20th century in noticing crucial similarities between Indo-European languages and other families across the Eurasian landmass. A group of Russian scholars' version of this refers to a grand *Nostratic* family; Greenberg and Ruhlen differ in exactly which families they include but agree in broad outline.

  B. Their *Eurasiatic* family includes Indo-European, Uralic (including Finnish and Hungarian), Altaic (stretching across Asia and including Turkish and Mongolian), Korean and Japanese, the Chukchi-Kamchatkan group spoken in far eastern Russia, and the Eskimo-Aleut languages spoken across the Bering Strait in northern North America.

  C. Evidence that these families had a common ancestor comes from similarities such as those outlined below.

Evidence for the Eurasiatic mega-family:

	I, me, my	you (sing.)	who	what
Indo-European	*mē	*tu	*kwi	*ma
Uralic	*-m	*te	*ke	*mi
Turkic	men		*kim	*mi
Mongolian	mini	*ti	ken	*ma
Korean	-ma		-ka	mai
Chukchi-Kamchatkan	-m	-t	*kina	*mi
Eskimo-Aleut	-ma	-t	*kina	*mi

D. Note that words for "I" beginning with *m* and words for "you" beginning with *t*—a pattern we are familiar with from Spanish (*me/te*)—are common across Asia and in the Arctic. Importantly, similarities between aspects of grammar, rather than concrete words, are considered more indicative of a historical relationship because grammatical items change more slowly than concrete ones. For example, Russian's noun and verb endings are similar to Latin's in both their shape and function, while its vocabulary is extremely different.

II. Smaller superfamilies: Amerind.

A. Of the dozens of language groups spoken by Native Americans in the New World, Greenberg, supported by Ruhlen, classified them into just three groups: two small ones in the north, Eskimo-Aleut and Na-Dené, and an enormous one encompassing all of the others, which he called *Amerind*.

B. One piece of evidence for Amerind is a particular word shape referring to family members of the same age or younger than oneself, *t—na*, with the vowel changing according to sex. Variations on this pattern are found throughout the New World languages and are unlikely to be accidental.

Evidence for the Amerind family:

t'ina "son, brother"   *t'una* "daughter, sister"   *t'ana* "child, sibling"

Iranshe *atina*   Iranshe *atuna*
"male relative"   "female relative"

Tiquie *ten*   Tiquie *ton*
"son"   "daughter"

Yurok *tsin*   Salinan *a-t'on*   Nootka *t'an'a*
"young man"   "younger sister"   "child"

Mohawk *-tsin*   Tacana *-tóna*   Aymara *tayna*
"male, boy"   "younger sister"   "first-born child"

C. Lately, genetic evidence has supported an Amerind family, showing that Native Americans' genetic patterns differ exactly according to the three groups Greenberg identified.

D. Specialists in Native American languages have objected that the evidence for Amerind as a language group is a collection of chance correspondences and that anyone could find a similar range of chance correspondences to "prove" any classification. Ruhlen objects that it would be impossible to make a case for a *t—na root with these vowel changes from the world's languages beyond Amerind—and he has a point.

III. How much does time bury?

   A. Recently, Ruhlen has documented close affinities between an obscure language of Nepal, Kusunda, generally classified as related to Chinese (Sino-Tibetan) and the language family of Papua New Guinea, called *Indo-Pacific*. Here are some common features between Kusunda and one of the languages of this group, Juwoi.

   Evidence for the relationship between Kusunda and Indo-Pacific languages:

	KUSUNDA	JUWOI
I	tˢi	tui
my	tˢi-yi	tii-ye
you	nu	ŋui
your	ni-yi	ŋii-ye
give	ai	a
this	(y)it	ete
knee	tugutu	togar ("ankle")
unripe	katuk	kadak ("bad character")

   B. This relationship is crucial because humans are known to have traveled from southern Asia to New Guinea at least 50,000 years ago, with recent evidence suggesting as long as 75,000 years ago. Thus, these words may represent the oldest documentable historical relationship between words and show that many linguists' claim that no relationship between languages can be documented beyond 6,000 or so years is untenable.

IV. Final verdict.

   A. Ruhlen's point that comparative reconstruction is not the only way to show that languages have a common ancestor is valid in itself. He observes that linguists posited the Indo-European group long before Proto-Indo-European itself had been worked out by working backward from the languages. The similarities between language families are close enough that his point is likely valid for mega-groups, such as Amerind and Eurasiatic.

B. A question still remains, however, as to how realistic even this approach is for Proto-World. The issues could be resolved as more proto-languages are reconstructed, although work of this kind is done increasingly less by modern linguists, and for reasons we will see in later lectures, it may be entirely impossible to reconstruct proto-languages for many families.

Essential Reading:

Ruhlen, Merritt. *The Origin of Language: Tracing the Evolution of the Mother Tongue*. New York: John Wiley & Sons, 1994.

———. "Taxonomic Controversies in the Twentieth Century," in *New Essays on the Origin of Language*, edited by Jürgen Trabant and Sean Ward, pp. 97–214. Berlin: Mouton de Gruyter, 2001.

Questions to Consider:

1. Why do grammatical items, such as prefixes and suffixes, change more slowly than separate words do? Along the same lines, what kinds of words do you think might change more slowly than others?
2. The debate between the Proto-World school and other linguists is partly the product of the age-old divide between "lumpers" (attuned to broad patterns) and "splitters" (attuned to fine details). Is it the job of the academic to be a "splitter" and leave the lumping to laymen, or do you think that "lumping" has a place in academic thought as well?

Lecture Fourteen
Dialects—Subspecies of Species

Scope: When the process that turns one language into a number of new ones has not yet gone far enough to create new languages per se, then the variations are considered *dialects* of the original language. This is what dialects are: variations on a common theme, rather than bastardizations of a "legitimate" standard variety. England is home to a number of variations on English, and importantly, Standard English is just another dialect that developed alongside these and happened to be chosen as the "show" dialect. The Parisian dialect of French was anointed in similar fashion. Often, what is considered the "proper" dialect today is a mere "dialect" tomorrow, such as Provençal in France.

Outline

I. Variety within languages.
  A. "Language" is, strictly speaking, an artificial, arbitrary concept. Not only has the first language developed into 6,000, but almost all of these languages are, viewed close up, bundles of variations on a theme. These are dialects of the languages.
  B. Here are some British dialects of English. Note that many are different enough from Standard English that they require translation.

STANDARD	The government has today decreed that all British beef is safe for consumption.
SCOTS	Efter he had gane throu the haill o it, a fell faimin brak out i yon laund.
	"After he had gone through all of it, a great famine broke out in the land."

LANCASHIRE	Ween meet neaw ta'en a hawse steyler at wur mayin' off with'tit.
	"We have just now taken a horse stealer who was making off with it."
NOTTINGHAMSHIRE	Tha mun come one naight ter th' cottage, afore tha goos; sholl ter?
	"You must come one night to the cottage before you go, will you?"
CORNWALL	Aw bain't gwine for tell ee.
	"He isn't going to tell you."

II. Ordinary language change creates dialects.

    A. We can understand what dialects are only by shedding the common misconception that a dialect is a degraded version of the standard language. What creates dialects is not sloth but simple language change.

    B. Recall how several languages can develop from one, as the Romance languages did from Latin.

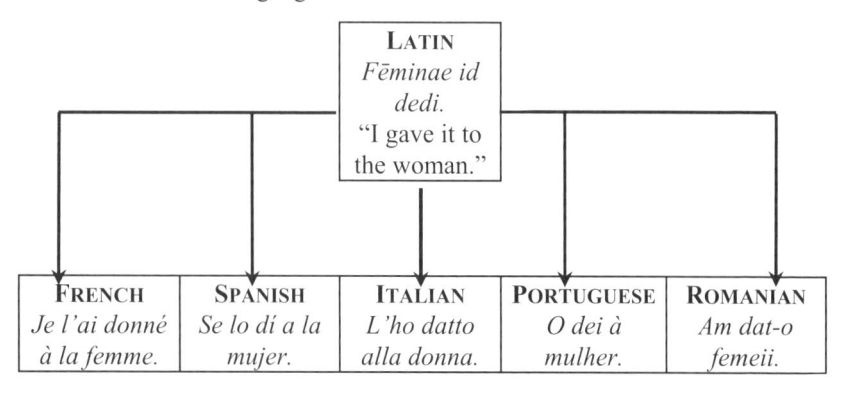

LATIN
Fēminae id dedi.
"I gave it to the woman."

FRENCH	SPANISH	ITALIAN	PORTUGUESE	ROMANIAN
Je l'ai donné à la femme.	*Se lo dí a la mujer.*	*L'ho datto alla donna.*	*O dei à mulher.*	*Am dat-o femeii.*

    C. Dialects are simply the intermediate stage in this process: at a certain point, a language has changed in several directions into new varieties that are not divergent enough to be different languages altogether but are obviously on their way.

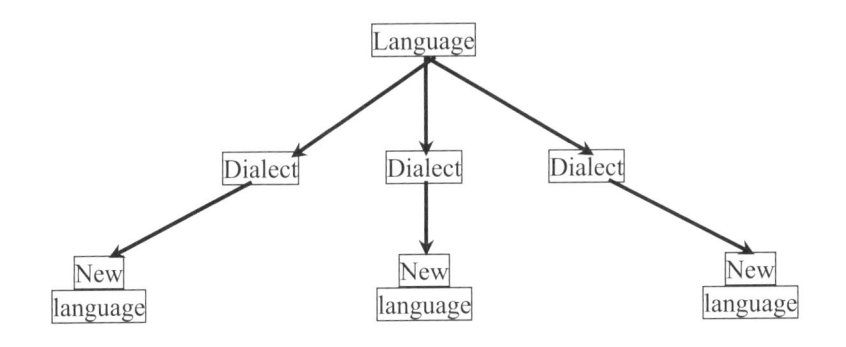

```
        Language
       /   |    \
   Dialect Dialect Dialect
      |      |       |
    New    New     New
  language language language
```

D. We have records of French, for example, at an intermediate stage between Latin and its current state. At that point, one writer complained in 63 A.D.:

Spoken Latin has picked up a passel of words considered too casual for written Latin, and the grammar people use when speaking has broken down. The masses barely use anything but the nominative and the accusative... it's gotten to the point that the student of Latin is writing in what is to them an artificial language, and it is an effort for him to recite in it decently. (Monteilhet, H. *Neropolis: Roman des temps néroniens*. Paris: Éditions du Juillard, 1984.)

E. Here is an example of the same sentence in several different English dialects:

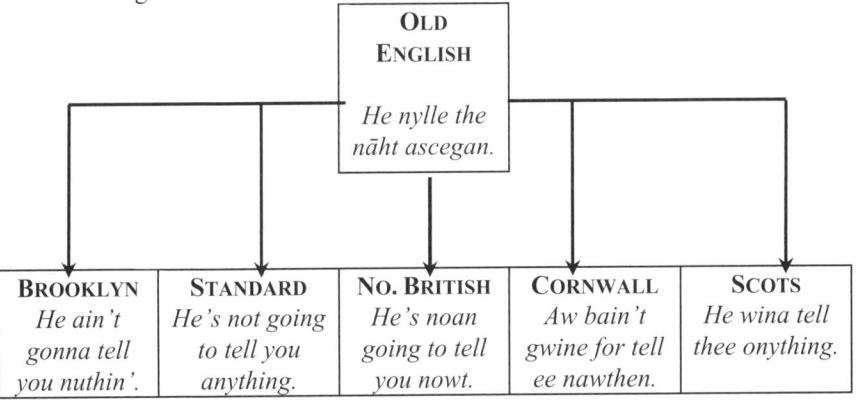

OLD ENGLISH

He nylle the nāht ascegan.

BROOKLYN	STANDARD	NO. BRITISH	CORNWALL	SCOTS
He ain't gonna tell you nuthin'.	*He's not going to tell you anything.*	*He's noan going to tell you nowt.*	*Aw bain't gwine for tell ee nawthen.*	*He wina tell thee onything.*

- **F.** Most languages are bundles of dialects like this.
    1. English borrowed *warrant* from French, but in Standard French, the word is *garant*. *Warrant* is borrowed from the Normandy dialect, which often had *w* where Standard French has *g*.
    2. Italian dialects are so different from one another that the dialect of Sicily is essentially a different language from the standard.
    3. The situation is similar in Germany. In Standard German, "You have something" is *Du hast etwas*; in a southern dialect, Schwäbisch, it is *De hesch oppis*.

III. The standard is just lucky.
- **A.** When a language is a written one, one of the dialects is usually chosen as the standard dialect, used in writing and public contexts. But an important thing to notice is that standard dialects usually develop alongside nonstandard ones, rather than the nonstandard ones developing from the standard.
- **B.** "A standard is a dialect with an army and a navy"—standards become standard because they have "the juice" in some way. Francien French became predominant because the national courts settled in its region; Castillian Spanish because it was spoken by the armies who advanced southward to defeat the Moors; Tuscan Italian because that region produced Dante, Petrarch, and Boccaccio.
- **C.** Standard English is the dialect that happened to be spoken in the region where London was. Before this, England was a patchwork of very different dialects. In the late 1400s, printer William Caxton told a story of a Londoner who had barely been able to make himself understood in Kent, the region just next door, because he had asked for *eggs* instead of using the Kentish dialect word, *eyren*.
- **D.** France was also once home to many distinct dialects. This was seen as a problem as France coalesced from a patchwork of feudal duchies into a nation. The Abbé Grégoire, a Catholic priest and revolutionary, worried in 1789 that:

France is home to perhaps 8 million subjects of which some can barely mumble a few malformed words or one or two disjointed sentences of our language: the rest know none at all. We know that in Lower Brittany, and beyond the Loire, in many places, the clergy is still obliged to preach in the local patois, for fear, if they spoke French, of not being understood. (Grillo, Ralph. *Dominant Languages: Language and Hierarchy in Britain and France.* Cambridge: Cambridge University Press, 1989, p. 31.)

The dialect of French that had developed in the Paris area was imposed on the population for practical reasons.

E. *Standard today, dialect tomorrow.* Ukrainian and Russian are similar enough that for a Russian, learning Ukrainian straddles the boundary between learning a new language and adjusting to a variety of Russian itself. Indeed, before the Ukraine was cordoned off as a separate region in the Soviet Union, it was a region within Russia, and the speech of the Ukraine was considered a kind of "Russian." When the center of power in Russia was Kiev, the speech of the Ukraine was considered the "best" Russian. After this, however, Ukrainian was dismissed as the speech of peasants. Then, when the Ukraine became a political entity, Ukrainian again became a "language." The difference had been in culture and politics, not in the speech variety itself.

IV. The standard seems "better" only because of accident. Dialects are equivalent to subspecies in the animal and plant kingdoms. Scots, Brooklyn English, and Standard English are to "English" as cocker spaniel, dachshund, and collie are to "dog." Just as there is no "default" or unequivocally "best" dog, there is no "real" dialect of a language. Rather, dialects are evidence of the variety-within-the-variety among the descendants of the first language.

Essential Reading:

Crystal, David. *The Cambridge Encyclopedia of the English Language.* Cambridge: Cambridge University Press, 1995 (especially chapter 5: "Early Modern English").

McWhorter, John H. *Word on the Street: Debunking the Myth of a "Pure" Standard English.* New York: Perseus, 1998.

Supplementary Reading:

Grillo, Ralph. *Dominant Languages: Language and Hierarchy in Britain and France.* Cambridge: Cambridge University Press, 1989.

Questions to Consider:

1. Often, people come away from a lecture like this one nevertheless still quite convinced that certain ways of speaking are just "incorrect." If by chance you feel this way, explore the difference between "nonstandard" and "incorrect" and how this justifies your sense of proper and improper language.

2. Generally, even speakers of nonstandard dialects consider their way of speaking "not real language." But if the way they speak evolved alongside the standard variety based on the same processes, then what conditions this sense of what "real" language is? Do you agree or disagree with this sense?

Lecture Fifteen
Dialects—Where Do You Draw the Line?

Scope: The labels *language* and *dialect* are, in practice, arbitrary, and necessarily so. Dialects of one language can be called separate languages simply because they are spoken in different countries, such as Swedish, Norwegian, and Danish. Different languages can be called dialects because they are spoken in the same country and written in the same system, such as Chinese "dialects," which are as different as French and Spanish. Often, dialects change slightly from region to region until people at one end of the chain cannot converse with people on the other end; where one draws the line between dialect and language here becomes meaningless.

The truth is that there is no such thing in any definable sense as a "language." Tens of thousands of dialects are spread across the globe, many of them akin enough to be perceptible as variations on "the same thing"—but even here, only in variable degrees.

Outline

I. Dialects as "languages": Often what begins being considered a dialect of one language is recast as a separate "language" of its own when its speakers are incorporated into a new nation.

  A. *Scandinavian.* Swedish, Norwegian, and Danish are official languages of Sweden, Norway, and Denmark. But speakers of them can manage a conversation, and on the page, they reveal themselves as minor variations on a pattern, rather like Scots, Cornwall English, and Standard English.

  The Danes initially ruled Sweden and Norway, and there was no such thing as a Swedish "language" until Sweden became independent in 1526 or a Norwegian "language" until Norway became independent in 1814. Until their independence, Sweden and Norway's speech varieties were simply considered dialects of Danish.

  B. *Moldovan.* Romania used to extend eastward into a little hump of land called Moldova. At first, the speech of Moldova was considered one of many nonstandard dialects of Romanian. But after Moldova was incorporated into the Soviet Union, the Soviets directed Moldovan linguists to write grammars of a new Moldovan "language," even though many of these were just grammars of Romanian translated into Russian.

C. *Different culture, different language?* Hindi is spoken in India and written in the Devanagari script, while Urdu is spoken in Pakistan and written in Arabic script. Because of this and the religious and political tensions between the countries, Hindi and Urdu are treated as separate "languages" when they are, in fact, the same one. Hindi has more Sanskrit borrowings, while Urdu has more from Arabic, but these impede communication little more than the differences between American and British English.

D. *Indigenous languages.* The continuum nature of the language/dialect distinction is clear even when the speech varieties are not adopted as written languages and assigned by nations as single official ones.

  1. *Malinke, Bambara, and Dyula in West Africa.* The "languages" Malinke and Bambara are spoken in a vast region spread across such West African countries as Senegal, Mali, and Guinea, alongside dozens of other languages in each country. But speakers of these languages can understand one another, as well as speakers of the Dyula "language" in Côte d'Ivoire. Only cultural affiliations determine what this one "language" is called from place to place.

  2. *Tourai and Aria in New Guinea.* On the island of New Britain near New Guinea, there are two groups called the Tourai and the Aria. What the two groups speak appears to be the same language with minor differences on the page, and other peoples in the area learn the same language to speak to both. But while the Tourai think of the Aria as speaking a different language, the Aria think of themselves as speaking the same thing as the Tourai.

II. Languages as "dialects": In other cases, separate languages are treated as dialects of one because they are all spoken in one nation or by the same cultural group.

A. *Chinese.* As we have seen, Chinese "dialects," such as Mandarin and Cantonese, are actually as different as the Romance languages are from one another.

B. Obviously these are separate languages, and the five other main Chinese "dialects" are just as different from one another, such as Taiwanese and Shanghainese. But all of the languages are written with the same system, which uses symbols for whole words instead of for sounds. This means that the languages look quite similar to one another on the page, since, for example, the word for *man* is the same symbol in all of the languages even though the spoken word is quite different. Then, the sense that all of the languages' speakers have of being united as "Chinese" completes the impression that there is a single Chinese "language."

C. *Arabic*. The varieties of what is called "Arabic" in various nations are as different as the Romance languages as well.

nothing in Arabic "dialects":

Algerian	ši
Tunisian	šay
Nigerian	še
Moroccan	wálu
Saudi	walašay
Egyptian	dilwa'ti
Libyan	kān lbarka

But these languages are largely used only for speaking. Modern Standard Arabic, based on the language of the Koran, is used in writing and formal language in most of these countries, and the spoken variety is considered a bastard version of the standard rather than as a separate "language" in its own right. Hence, there is a sense that one language, "Arabic," is spoken across the Arab world, rather than several different languages.

III. Dialect continua: The distinction between language and dialect is ever more hopeless when we see that in many parts of the world, one dialect shades into another one from region to region until people on one end of the chain speak a different "language" than the ones at the other, but there has been no single point along the chain where a new language can be seen as beginning.

A. *Gurage*. Gurage is the name of a dialect continuum of the Semitic family, spoken in Ethiopia. Here is "He thatched a roof" in several of the varieties, shading gradually from one "language" to another.

He thatched a roof in Gurage dialects

Soddo	kəddənəm
Gogot	kəddənəm
Muher	khəddənəm
Ezha	khəddərəm
Chaha	khədərəm
Gyeto	khətərə
Endegen	həttərə

People speaking one variety can converse with people speaking the one next door, have a harder time with the one spoken two regions away, and so on. Soddo and Endegen seem easily identifiable as "languages," but whether, for example, Chaha in the middle is a different "language" from either of them is as arbitrary an issue as whether purple is more red or more blue.

B. *Turkic varieties.* Turkish is one of a litter of languages stretching from Turkey east across the new "stan" countries into western China. These "languages" vary in the same way as what are called "dialects" of many other languages and form a continuum. Here is the word for *eight* stretching from west to east.

eight in Turkic languages

Turkish	sekiz
Azerbaijani	səkkiz
Turkmen	sekiz
Uzbek	sakkiz
Kazakh	segiz
Kirghiz	segiz
Uighur	säkkiz

Yet the Gurage varieties are thought of as "dialects," while these are "languages"—the terminology is arbitrary, based largely on the fact that the Turkic ones are spoken in separate political entities.

IV. Dialect of A or new language B?

A. Even when there is no continuum of this kind, the question of whether one speech variety is a dialect of one language or a new language entirely is often undecidable.

B. Scots English can test the comprehension of an English speaker. Consider that *auld lang syne* means *old long since*. But hearing Scots spoken at speed in casual situations, an English speaker is often confronted with what feels like an ill-tuned radio signal. This is an experience typical of speakers of most languages: English is unique in how few speech varieties straddle the line between it and other languages.

Essential Reading:

The topic of this lecture is not generally covered in sources for a general audience. With all due humility, I believe that the most pertinent survey of the topic of this lecture is my own: McWhorter, John. *The Power of Babel.* New York: HarperCollins, 2001 (chapter 2).

Supplementary Reading:

These are some language area surveys that those interested might find useful:

Arabic: Versteegh, Kees. *The Arabic Language*. New York: Columbia University Press, 1997.

Chinese: Norman, Jerry. *Chinese*. Cambridge: Cambridge University Press, 1988.

Moldovan: Dyer, Donald L. *The Romanian Dialect of Moldova*. Lewiston, NY: Mellen Press, 1999.

Scots: Crystal, David. *The Cambridge Encyclopedia of the English Language*. Cambridge: Cambridge University Press, 1995 ("Middle Scots," pp. 52–53; "Variation in Scotland," pp. 328–333).

Questions to Consider:

1. After this lecture, do you perhaps have a sense that there is any salvaging of the distinction between language and dialect that rises above the messy reality?

2. Arabic as spoken from country to country differs as much as the Romance languages do, but the writing system helps all of the peoples in question see themselves as speaking one "Arabic." The Chinese "dialects" are similar. Are speech varieties that share a writing system "the same language"? How important is writing to defining what a "language" is?

Lecture Sixteen
Dialects—Two Tongues in One Mouth

Scope: In most Arabic-speaking countries, the Arabic of public use (the media, speeches, writing) is essentially a different language from the one used casually and learned from parents. This phenomenon is called *diglossia* and is common worldwide. Swiss German speakers only occasionally see the language they speak on the page, where High German is required. Different languages are also often used in diglossic relationships: the Tanzanian often uses English and Swahili at work and a local native language at home. Diglossia is the template within which 6,000 languages and countless dialects share space on a planet with only 200-odd nations.

The nonstandard dialect and the standard one often coexist in a structured relationship in a society. The standard or "high" (H) variety is used in formal situations, while the nonstandard or "low" (L) variety is used in informal ones. This is called *diglossia*, Greek for "two tongues."

Outline

I. Typical examples: Modern Standard Arabic versus Egyptian Arabic; High German versus Swiss German in Switzerland; Katharévousa versus Dhimotikí in Greece.

II. Typical traits of diglossia.

A. *Writing versus speaking.* People read the paper in H and discuss the issues in L. Speeches are given in H; conversations are conducted in L.

B. *Acquisition.* H is learned in school; L is learned at home.

C. *Standardization.* H is standardized with official "rules," while nonstandard varieties are described systematically only by academic linguists, missionaries, and similar researchers. This lack of standardization often encourages several L's to arise, such as the many nonstandard dialects of German.

D. *Prestige*. People tend to disown that they speak L, or do not consider L a "real language" (there were riots in Greece in 1903 over the publication of the New Testament in Dhimotikí).

III. Typical examples.

A. *Egyptian Arabic*. In Egyptian Arabic, "now" is *dilwa'ti*; in Standard Arabic, it is *'al'āna*. Egyptian Arabic for "nose" is *manaxīr*; in Standard Arabic, it is *'anf*. In other cases, the Egyptian is a variation on the standard: "many" is *kathirah* in Standard, *kətir* in Egyptian. An Egyptian learns to speak, essentially, a whole new language in school.

B. *Swiss German*. In German-speaking Switzerland, to be a functioning person requires being bilingual in two forms of "German" that are as different as Spanish and Portuguese. High German for "drink" is *trinken*; Swiss German has *suufe*. High German has *kein* for "not one"; Swiss German has *ke*.

C. *Triglossia*. In particularly hierarchical societies, there can be three levels of language according to context. In Javanese, for example, there is a "middle rung" between the "highest" and "lowest" forms. Here is "Are you going to eat rice and cassava now?" on all three levels.

HIGH	menapa	pandjenengan	badé	ḍahar
MIDDLE	napa	sampéjan	adjeng	neḍa
LOW	apa	kowé	arep	mangan
	Are	you	going	to eat

HIGH	sekul	kalijan	kaspé	samenika?
MIDDLE	sekul	lan	kaspé	saniki?
LOW	sega	lan	kaspé	saiki?
	rice	and	cassava	now

D. The closest equivalent to diglossia in English is the difference between such words as *dine* and *eat*, *children* and *kids*, or *parcels* and *bags*. Imagine if differences like these applied to most of the words in the language!

IV. Diglossia of languages.
- **A.** There are about 6,000 languages in the world and only 200-odd countries; this shows that multilingualism in nations is a norm.
- **B.** The appearance otherwise is explained by the fact that only a quarter of the world's countries recognize two languages officially, and only four recognize three or more. India recognizes Hindi, English, and 14 regional languages; Singapore: Chinese, Malay, Tamil, and English; Spain: Spanish, Catalan, and Basque; and Luxembourg: French, German, and the local German dialect Letzebuergesch.
- **C.** Languages typically share space in a country in diglossic relationships. An example is Paraguay, where the official languages are Spanish and the Native American language Guaraní. But the two languages are not simply used side by side in all contexts. Guaraní is used as the L language and Spanish as the H one.
- **D.** In fact, where there is extensive bilingualism, diglossia is almost inevitable.
    1. In Quebec before 1974, English was the H language and French the L one. But in the 1970s, a law was enacted that made French the province's official language and required the use of French in the government and on public signs. This has been a delicate and charged situation, imposed rather than emerging by itself.
    2. Although extensive bilingualism without diglossia is rare, diglossia can exist among an elite in a society even when most of the society's people are not bilingual. In Czarist Russia, upper-class people often spoke French among themselves, especially on formal occasions. French was the H and Russian was the L.

Essential Reading:

Ferguson, Charles A. *Language Structure and Language Use* (essays selected and introduced by Anwar S. Dil). Palo Alto, CA: Stanford University Press, 1971 ("Diglossia" essay).

Supplementary Reading:

Geertz, Clifford. "Linguistic Etiquette," in *Sociolinguistics*, edited by John Pride and Janet Holmes, pp. 167–179. Harmondsworth, England: Penguin, 1972.

Questions to Consider:

1. Is extreme diglossia, such as in Arabic-speaking countries, a problem? Would it be better if spoken languages were used in formal contexts as well, or is there an advantage to the existence of a "common coin" that unites all such countries?

2. What are some words or expressions that we regularly say but rarely write, such as "whole nother"? You will find that there is more diglossia in modern English than we are often aware of.

Lecture Seventeen
Dialects—The Standard as Token of the Past

Scope: Languages typically change quite quickly: there are cases where linguists examine a language at one point only to find that 60 years later, it has morphed into practically a brand new one. However, when a dialect of a language is used widely in writing and literacy is high, the pace of change is artificially slowed because people come to see "the language" as on the page and inviolable. This helps create diglossia: standard Arabic is based on the language of the Koran, while the colloquial Arabics went on with natural change.

Outline

I. The normal speed of language change.

  A. When linguists studied the northern Australian language Ngan'gityemerri in 1930, they found a language with sentences similar to the following:

  1930:
  Dudu dam, dam dudu,   kinji   dinj   parl.
  Track poke poke track   here   he-sat   camp

  "He poked along, tracking it along here to where it made its camp."

  1990:
  Damdudu, damdudu,   kinyi   dinyparl.
  Poke-track poke-track here   he-sat-camp

  Notice that in 1930 the speaker could give the order of *dudu* and *dam* (*track* and *poke*) in either order; they were separate words. But when linguists returned to the language in 1990, its entire grammar had changed. Now, *dudu* had grammaticalized into a prefix of *dam*, such that there was one word *dududam*, meaning roughly "pokingly tracked." This had happened with all verbs in the language. Ngan'gityemerri had moved along the path toward becoming a language like Yupik Eskimo, which packs a sentence's worth of meaning into one word. (Recall the Yupik Eskimo word for "He had not yet said again that he was going to hunt reindeer": *Tuntussuqatarniksaitengqiggtuq*.)

B. But English has changed more slowly in the time after the Middle Ages. Shakespeare speaking 500 years ago would have sounded strange to us, but we could converse with him. However, Shakespeare would have found an Old English speaker from 500 years earlier almost as incomprehensible as a German.

C. This phenomenon can be explained by the fact that when a language is written and standardized and literacy becomes widespread, the written form comes to be seen as "The Language," and it affects people's speaking habits enough that the language changes more slowly than it would naturally. Standardized languages are "frozen in aspic," as it were.

D. A contrast: we can easily read presidential addresses from the late 18th century, but a speaker of Saramaccan Creole in Suriname would find the speech of a chief in 1789 extremely peculiar. For example, at that time, the way to say "not" was *no*, but today, it is just *a*.

II. Standard languages and diglossia.

A. When a standard language is "frozen" in place while the spoken language develops naturally, often the result is diglossia between the standard and the colloquial variety.

B. This was the case with Arabic. For example, the regional Arabic dialects are the result of natural changes Arabic went through over time in each place, while the standard reflects the archaic language of the Koran.

  1. Notice that the contrast between standard *kathirah* and Egyptian *kətir* shows the erosion of sounds at the ends of words, just as we pronounce name as "NEIGHM" rather than "NAH-muh," the earlier form of the word that the spelling preserves.

  2. Modern Standard Arabic has three case endings: "house" is *bayt**u***, "of the house" is *bayt**i***, and when "house" is used as an object, it is *bayt**a***. But in Egyptian, these endings have disappeared, because sound erosion wore off final vowels, as it does so often in language change.

C. Notice also that the words for "are" in the levels of Javanese from the previous lecture show the same kind of development:

"Are you going to eat rice and cassava now?"

HIGH	menapa	pandjenengan		badé	dahar
MIDDLE	napa	sampéjan		adjeng	neḍa
LOW	apa	kowé		arep	mangan
	Are	you		going	to eat

HIGH	sekul	kalijan	kaspé	samenika?
MIDDLE	sekul	lan	kaspé	saniki?
LOW	sega	lan	kaspé	saiki?
	rice	and	cassava	now

The word for *now*, *samenika* in the high variety, becomes *saniki* and *saiki*.

D. Standard French versus colloquial French.
1. Although Standard French has a double-negative marking, as in *Je **ne** marche **pas***, "I do not walk," in spoken French, the *ne* is almost always dropped: *Je marche pas* has been good spoken French since the Middle Ages. Small words, such as *ne*, that are not accented tend to erode and even disappear in languages, just as sounds at the ends of words do. Spoken French has developed "naturally," while written French preserves a past stage.
2. French has a pronoun *on* used generically, equivalent to the *se* in *Aquí se habla español*, or *one* in English. But over the centuries, although *nous* has been the standard form for "we," *on* has been used in its place in casual speech. We are taught to say *nous parlons* for "we speak," but French people at all levels of society actually say *on parle*.

That is the only thing that we do not do.

STANDARD FRENCH:
C'est la seule chose que **nous ne** faisons pas.

SPOKEN FRENCH:
C'est la seule chose qu'**on** __ fait pas.

3. This means that to learn to speak French, we must learn a different dialect than the one taught in school—there are two Frenches, the standard that reflects what French was like centuries ago and the spoken version that has evolved since then.

III. The standard is not always more complex.
   A. Because nonstandard dialects lose material over time, it can appear that the standard must really be the "better" version because it retains these things, and thus is "larger" than the nonstandard dialects.
   B. But actually, languages complexify as they evolve while they are simplifying. This has happened in regional Arabic dialects, such as Egyptian. For example, Standard Arabic is fairly simple in terms of showing differences in time conceptions. Basically, there is a past and a present: "he wrote" is *kataba*; "he writes" is *yaktubu*. The future, the progressive, and so on are usually left to context.
   C. But Egyptian, like other regional Arabic varieties, has developed markers to indicate time distinctions. For example, in Saudi Arabic, one places *b-* before a verb to indicate the future: *aguul*, "I tell"; *baguul*, "I will tell." *Kaan* before a verb means "used to": *kaan aguul*, "I used to tell."

Essential Reading:

The most pertinent exposition on this subject for the general reader is, honestly: McWhorter, John. *The Power of Babel*. New York: HarperCollins, 2001 (chapter 6).

Questions to Consider:

1. Is language change a bad thing? It often seems so in real life as we live it ("Why are people using *impact* as a verb?"). But Shakespeare played a major part in changing our language. Are there good changes versus bad ones, and what is the difference?
2. In Black English, *be* is used to indicate a habitual action: "She be goin to the store every Tuesday." This is a more explicit way of marking habituality than Standard English's simple "She goes to the store every Tuesday." Indeed, the *be* is "unconjugated," but in your opinion, does that render this usage of *be* "wrong" even if it also lends the dialect some clarity?

Lecture Eighteen
Dialects—Spoken Style, Written Style

Scope: We often see the written style of language as how it really "is" or "should be." But in fact, writing allows uses of language that are impossible when a language is only a spoken one, which all but about 200 of the world's languages effectively are. Writing allows the preservation of a massive vocabulary in dictionaries: spoken languages have some tens of thousands of words at most. Writing allows longer, more elaborate sentences than are typical of speech anywhere in the world. Early writing, such as the Hebrew Bible with its brief phrases, represents speech rather than the artifice of writing.

A main reason that standard varieties appear to be "realer" than nonstandard ones is that they have a richer vocabulary and more elaborated syntax. But it is important to realize that this trait is an artificial imposition from technology on the natural history of human language.

Outline

I. Spoken language: Raggedy but effective.

  A. In the lecture, we hear part of a speech by Congressman Adam Clayton Powell, Jr. from the late 1960s, in the fundamentalist preaching style. As majestic as this passage is, its structure and language are rather simple. Sentences are short and repetitive. A composition teacher, if presented with the passage in writing, would likely advise the writer to use some graceful transitional words to knit the sentences together, such as *although*, *seeing that*, etc.

  B. But this is how language is spoken casually worldwide. Standard English often comes in prose of this kind from Gibbon's *The Decline and Fall of the Roman Empire*:

  The whole engagement lasted above twelve hours, till the gradual retreat of the Persians was changed into a disorderly flight, of which the shameful example was given by the principal leaders and the Surenas himself. They were pursued to the gates of Ctesiphon, and the conquerors might have entered the dismayed city, if their general,

Victor, who was dangerously wounded with an arrow, had not conjured them to desist from such a rash attempt, which must be fatal if it were not successful. (Edward Gibbon, *The Decline and Fall of the Roman Empire*, 1776 [Volume I, chapter 24].)

Here, a single sentence stretches endlessly, in elaborate structure that a composition teacher would approve of.

C. But this kind of language is possible only because there is writing. Writing is conscious and slow, allowing the writer to carefully compose long sentences and the reader to process them. Spoken language occurs in real time and generally occurs in packets of, on average, seven words.

D. If language had existed for 24 hours, then writing would have existed only since about 11:08 P.M. Only about 200 out of the 6,000 languages are "written" in the true sense of being used in official documents and having a literature. The elaborate traits of written language are a historical accident.

II. Spoken versus written language.

    A. *Vocabulary*. Spoken language makes use of a more limited vocabulary than written language. This is partly because writing allows the preservation of words over time. In spoken—that is, normal!—languages, old words die away.

        1. The Lokele of the Democratic Republic of the Congo use a talking-drum language that has many words no one recalls the meanings of. There is no dictionary to preserve them the way *ruth*—the root of *ruthless*—is preserved in English dictionaries.

        2. Spoken English makes use of a small subset of all the words in the language. Linguists Wallace Chafe and Jane Danielewicz have shown that even educated Americans use hedges to compensate for the difficulty of making maximal use of English vocabulary when speaking in real time, such as in this quote:

        She was still young enough so I… I just… was able to put her in an… uh—*sort of*… sling… I mean one of those tummy packs… you know.

        Languages only used orally tend to have thousands or maybe tens of thousands of words—not the hundreds of thousands that written languages hoard in dictionaries for eternal reference.

B. *Syntax.* Spoken language uses shorter, simpler sentences than written language. This is part of a folktale narrated by a speaker of Saramaccan Creole. Because this is spoken language, the sentences are rather short.

Anasi dɛ a wã kɔndɛ.
Anancy [the spider] was in a village.

Nɔɔ hɛ̃ wɛ wã mujɛɛ bi dɛ a di kɔndɛ nããndɛ.
And a woman was in the village there.

Nɔɔ di mujɛɛ, a pali di miii wã daka.
And the woman bore a child one day.

Nɔɔ di a pali, nɔɔ dee oto sɛmbɛ u di kɔndɛ, de a ta si ɛ̃ u soni.
And when she gave birth, the other people in the village didn't want to have anything to do with her.

Hɛ̃ wɛ a begi Gadu te a wei.
Then she prayed to the gods fervently.

Hɛ̃ wɛ a go a lio.
Then she went to the river.

Nɔɔ di a go a lio, dee Gadu ko dɛ̃ɛ̃ wã mujɛɛmii.
And when she went to the river, the gods gave her a girl-child.

III. Language goes from spoken to written.

A. Even in early written English, it is clear that the writers are still writing with significant influence from how a language is used in speech. Here is a passage from the first English printed book, namely William Caxton's prologue to *The Recuyell of the Historyes of Troy*. Note that it is structured rather like the Saramaccan passage, with short phrases following one after the other:

And afterward when I remeberyd my self of my symplenes and vnperfightnes that I had in bothe langages, that is to wete [wit] in Freshe and in Englisshe, for in France was I neuer, and was born and lerned myn Englissh in Kente in the Weeld, where I doubte not is spoken as brode and rude Englishh as is in ony place of Englond; & haue contynued by the space of xxx yere for the most parte in the contres of Braband, Flandres, Holand, and Zeland;... (William Caxton's prologue to *The Recuyell of the Historyes of Troy*, cited in:

Crystal, David. *The Cambridge Encyclopedia of the English Language*. Cambridge: Cambridge University Press, 1995, p. 57.)

B. A passage like this reflects the almost sobering reality of how we speak English, rather than write it. This is an exchange between two students in the 1970s, and one must admit that this indeed reflects casual spoken English, as opposed to how we write it:

A. On a tree. Carbon isn't going to do much for a tree really. Really. The only thing it can do is collect moisture. Which may be good for it. In other words in the desert you have the carbon granules which would absorb, collect moisture on top of them. Yeah. It doesn't help the tree but it protects, keeps the moisture in. Uh huh. Because then it just soaks up moisture. It works by the water molecules adhere to the carbon moleh, molecules that are in the ashes. It holds it on. And the plant takes it away from there.

B. Oh, I have an argument with you.

A. Yeah.

B. You know, you said how silly it was about my, uh, well, it's not a theory at all. That the more pregnant you are and you see spots before your eyes it's proven that it's the retention of the water.

A. Yeah, the water's just gurgling all your eyes.

(Carterette, Edward C., and Margaret Hubbard Jones. *Informal Speech*. Berkeley: University of California Press, 1974, p. 390.)

C. Only by "translation" can we transform spoken English into written, a form that would never emerge from any human being speaking any language naturally, as with this passage as presented by linguist M.A.K. Halliday:

Spoken version:

I had to wait, I had to wait till it was born and till it got to about eight or ten weeks of age, then I bought my first dachshund, a black-and-tan bitch puppy, as they told me I should have bought a bitch puppy to start off with, because if she wasn't a hundred percent good I could choose a top champion dog to mate her to, and then produce something that was good, which would be in my own kennel prefix.

Hypothetical written version:

Some eight or ten weeks after the birth saw my first acquisition of a dachshund, a black-and-tan bitch puppy. It seems that a bitch puppy would have been the appropriate initial purchase, because of the possibility of mating an imperfect specimen with a top champion dog, the improved offspring then carrying my own kennel prefix.

(Halliday, M.A.K. "Spoken and Written Modes of Meaning," in *Comprehending Oral and Written Language*, edited by Rosalind Horowitz and S. Jay Samuels. New York: Academic Press. 1987, p. 59.)

D. The roots of written language in spoken language can be seen in the earlier written documents of many languages.

   1. Here is the way the opening passage of the Bible is often written:

   In the beginning, when God created the heavens and the earth, the earth was a formless wasteland, and darkness covered the abyss, while a mighty wind swept over the waters. Then God said, "Let there be light," and there was light.

   2. But the original Hebrew version does not scan this way at all. Instead, it is written in short sentences, reflecting spoken language:

   Bereshit bara Elohim et hashamayim ve'et ha'arets.
   Veha'arets hayetah tohu vavohu
   vechoshech al-peney tehom veruach.
   Elohim merafechet al-peney hamayim.
   Vayomer Elohim yehi-or va-yehi-or.

   In the beginning God created the heavens and the earth.
   And the earth was formless and empty
   with darkness on the face of the depths.
   God's spirit moved on the water's surface.
   God said, "There shall be light" and light came into existence.

   The Hebrew Bible was written at a time when writing was relatively new, and the writer was still inclined to simply transcribe language as it was spoken.

IV. What we are conditioned to view as the "real" type of language is actually a technological luxury, allowed by the transcription of language onto the page. All but a few languages are used orally only, and as complex as they tend to be, they are spoken in small "word packets," juxtaposed with a certain freedom that relies on context as much as structure to convey meaning and with relatively small vocabularies. The *Oxford English Dictionary* and the prose of Milton are historical curiosities, departures from the "natural," similar to dogs that bring in the newspaper.

Essential Reading:

Ong, Walter. *Orality and Literacy: The Technologizing of the Word*. London: Routledge, 1982.

Supplementary Reading:

Chafe, Wallace, and Jane Danielewicz. "Properties of Spoken and Written Language," in *Comprehending Oral and Written Language*, edited by Rosalind Horowitz and S. Jay Samuels, pp. 83–112. New York: Academic Press, 1987.

Goody, Jack, and Ian Watt. "The Consequences of Literacy," in *Literacy in Traditional Societies*, edited by Jack Goody, pp. 27–84. Cambridge: Cambridge University Press, 1968.

Halliday, M. A. K. "Spoken and Written Modes of Meaning," in *Comprehending Oral and Written Language*, edited by Rosalind Horowitz and S. Jay Samuels, pp. 55–82. New York: Academic Press, 1987.

Questions to Consider:

1. Make a tape recording of you and some friends speaking casually, and listen to how choppy and unstructured casual speech actually is. Do you and your friends talk the ways books are written?

2. Listen to a passage of a stand-up comedian and "translate" it into formal, written English. Does the passage lose something in the translation, or would you rather that the comedian had phrased it the way you have written it?

Lecture Nineteen
Dialects—The Fallacy of Blackboard Grammar

Scope: Understanding language change and how languages differ helps us to see that many of the things that we are taught are "wrong" about speech are misanalyses. Grammarians of the 1600s and 1700s passed many of these conceptions down to us, assuming that all languages should be patterned after Latin and Greek (thus, no *Billy and me went to the store*), that language change is decay (thus requiring the retention of *whom*), and that grammar must make strictly logical sense (thus, a pox on *I ain't seen nothin'*).

Another artificial incursion into the natural history of language is that because of the influence of standard dialects, people who speak written languages are often taught that constructions that they produce spontaneously are "errors" that they must be taught out of. This is a prescriptivist approach to language, in contrast to the descriptivist approach that linguists take.

Outline

I. History of prescriptivism in English: Many of the linguistic habits we are taught to avoid were only identified as "errors" by two influential English grammars.

   A. Robert Lowth wrote *A Short Introduction to English Grammar* in 1762, and Lindley Murray followed in its footsteps with his *English Grammar* in 1794.

   B. Because English had grown from a lowly vernacular to a language of worldwide influence, Lowth and Murray saw themselves as helping prepare English for its new role by giving it more "rules." But they labored under various illusions that this course teaches us out of. The result was a realm of "blackboard grammar" caveats that, in truth, have no logical foundation.

II. Illusion 1: Latin and Greek are the "best" languages.

   A. Lowth and Murray thought that Latin and Greek were "better" than English because of their complex case endings. Actually, languages without endings, such as Chinese, are complex in other ways, including their tones, classifiers, sentence-final particles, and so on.

B. Thus, we are taught that *Billy and me went to the store* is "wrong" because *me* is a subject. However, only sometimes do languages neatly assign pronouns according to the subject/object distinction.

    1. Latin was one of those languages, where the subject *I* was *ego* and the object form was *mē*, and never would *mē* be used as a subject.

    2. But in a great many languages, two forms share the subject position, depending on the type of sentence. In French, one would say *Guillaume et **moi** sommes allés au magasin*, with the object form, not *Guillaume et **je** sommes allés au magasin*. No one complains about this in French.

    3. Even in English, it is impossible to apply the "subject" rule consistently. If someone asks "Who did that?" and you know that it was two people on the other side of the room, when you point them out you say "Them!" not "They!", even though it is they who did it, and thus, we are dealing with subject form.

III. Illusion 2: Language change is decay.

A. Because Modern English contrasts most immediately with Old English in having lost most of its noun and verb endings, it was natural for Lowth and Murray to suppose that language change always involves loss of features and should be resisted. We tend to harbor a similar feeling today, even though, as we have seen, languages create new material as they lose it.

B. This sense that case distinctions must be retained is why we are still taught to use *whom*.

    1. Notice that we must be *taught* to use it, because otherwise, *what* and *who* are no longer marked for three cases (genitive, dative, and accusative) as they once were.

    2. But we only retain *whom* because it was still perceptible in English when grammarians began standardizing it. *Whom* was actually a remnant of a full system that had died unmourned. If we are to say *Whom did he see?* then the question arises as to why we do not say *Wham did he give it?* for *Who did he give it to?*, because *wham* was the dative ("to-") form of *who* in Old English.

IV. Illusion 3: Language must be logical.
- **A.** We are often taught that "proper" language is logical in the sense of mathematics. But this is unrealistic: all languages are full of wrinkles that do not make strict logical sense, but whose meaning is clear nevertheless. The influence of such grammarians as Lowth and Murray has sometimes shunted Standard English into unnatural detours.
- **B.** *Double negatives.* Double negatives, such as *She ain't seen nobody*, are common worldwide: the Spaniard says **Nunca** *he visto* **nada** ("never have I seen nothing") for *I have never seen anything*.
  - **1.** Old English had double negatives:

    Ic ne can noht singan.

    I no can nothing sing

    "I can't sing anything."

  - **2.** But in the region where Standard English happened to be developing, there was an alternative construction using forms with *any*, such as *I haven't seen anything*. Even here, though, double negatives could still be used for emphasis, even in Shakespeare, where Falstaff in *Henry IV (II)* says, "There's never none of these demure boys come to any proof" (IV.iii.97).
  - **3.** Lowth, Murray and others, however, decided that "two negatives make a positive," and gave double negatives an air of slovenliness that has been permanent. But notice that every single nonstandard dialect of English uses double negatives worldwide, as do thousands of languages!
- **C.** *You was.* In other cases, applying logic of one sort even works against speakers trying to iron out a wrinkle in the grammar themselves.
  - **1.** There is a wrinkle in how Standard English treats *you* with the verb "to be." Why is the plural form *were* used even when *you* is singular?

    | I was | we were |
    | you **were** | you were |
    | he/she was | they were |

2. Many nonstandard English dialects iron this out by using the singular form *was* when *you* refers to one person. This makes for a tidier chart:

I was	we were
you **was**	you were
he/she was	they were

   3. Well into the 1800s, this was even a common construction in Standard American English. Here is a letter written by a man to his lady friend in the 1830s; the elegance of the language makes it clear that his *you was* is not a mistake, and he uses it often.

   Indeed, I know not one word you did say, for I was so perfectly astonished in the first place, to see you going home without appearing even to think of me, and then when I met you at the door to find out that you **was** angry with me, I knew not what to make of it. There were many people looking at us, and I knew it. (Cohen, Patricia Cline. *The Murder of Helen Jewett*. New York: Vintage, 1998, p. 244.)

   4. But Lowth and Murray considered this to be using *you* with the "wrong" form; thus, English speakers are taught out of being logical!

   D. Languages simply do not make perfect sense: if we say *I am*, then why do we say *aren't I* instead of *amn't I*?

V. Artful language versus blackboard grammar.

   A. Certainly there are grounds for being taught how to structure one's sentences effectively and for being taught the nuances of "written" vocabulary, such as the difference between *uninterested* and *disinterested*. However, a great deal of what we are taught as "proper" or even "better" expression is based on sheer myth.

   B. Thus, we must avoid supposing that part of the natural history of language entails that in developed civilizations, decadence, democratization, and overburdened school systems lead to the language "going to the dogs." Constructions that toddlers produce naturally, and that as adults we avoid as a conditioned reflex but often slip into in unguarded moments, are natural language, not mistakes.

Essential Reading:

Bryson, Bill. *The Mother Tongue: English and How It Got That Way*. New York: William Morrow and Co., 1990 (chapter 9: "Good English and Bad").

Crystal, David. *The Cambridge Encyclopedia of Language*. Cambridge: Cambridge University Press, 1987 ("The Prescriptive Tradition").

Supplementary Reading:

Pinker, Steven. *The Language Instinct*. New York: HarperPerennial, 1994 (chapter 12: "The Language Mavens").

Questions to Consider:

1. Since the Middle Ages, English speakers have been using such sentences as "Tell each student that they can hand in their paper at the office," rather than "Tell each student that he can hand in his paper at the office," in formal writing. Yet we are often told that this is "wrong." If Italians use their *lei* to mean both "she" and a formal "you," then can we uphold insisting that *they* must refer to the plural?

2. Given that saying "you was" when referring to one person would technically make more "sense" and be "clearer" than saying "you were," can you identify precisely what conditions our native sense that this would be taking it "too far"?

Lecture Twenty
Language Mixture—Words

Scope: The first language's 6,000 branches have not only diverged into dialects but have constantly been mixing with one another on all levels. The level of words is the first: most of English's vocabulary is borrowed from Viking invaders, French rulers, and Latin and Greek. This is a common situation: 30 percent of Vietnamese's words are from Chinese. Often words are borrowed as "high" versions of native ones: thus English *pig* and French *pork*. This kind of word mixture is the essence of Spanglish today, although seeing the process at close hand often occasions discomfort.

So far, I have implied that the first language has developed like a bush, with a single sprout branching into a mass of twigs decorated with leaves. But this metaphor can take us only so far, because in actuality, languages and dialects have mixed with one another constantly. The relationship between the world's languages is analogous to a stew.

Languages mix to various extents. In this lecture, we will examine how they mix on the level of words (which is only the first, and least transformative, level possible).

Outline

I. The bastard vocabulary of English.

A. *The dictionary experience.* We English speakers are accustomed to finding that words in our language trace to Dutch, Greek, French, Latin, and other languages. It is almost the unexpected case that a word will simply trace directly back to Old English. Yet the Pole, for example, finds that many more of the words in his language proportionately trace back to Proto-Slavic.

B. Indeed, out of all of the words in the *Oxford English Dictionary*, no less than 99 percent were taken from other languages. The relative few that trace back to Old English itself are also 62 percent of the words most used, such as *and*, *but*, *father*, *love*, *fight*, *to*, *will*, *should*, *not*, *from*, and so on. Yet the vast majority of our vocabulary originated in foreign languages, including not merely the obvious "Latinate" items, like *adjacent*, but common, mundane forms not processed by us as "continental" in the slightest.

C. For example, every single word in that last sentence longer than three letters originated outside of English itself!

D. Main sources of borrowed words in English.
   1. *Vikings*. Vikings invaded and settled in the northern half of Britain starting in 787; they spoke Old Norse (ancestor of today's Scandinavian languages) and scattered about a thousand words into English, including such staples as *both*, *same*, *again*, *get*, *give*, *are*, *skirt*, *sky*, and *skin*.
   2. *Normans*. In 1066, French speakers took over England for roughly the next 200 years and introduced no fewer than about 7,500 words, including such ordinary words as *air*, *coast*, *debt*, *face*, *flower*, *joy*, *people*, *river*, *sign*, *blue*, *clear*, *easy*, *large*, *mean*, *nice*, *poor*, *carry*, *change*, *cry*, *move*, *push*, *save*, *trip*, *wait*, *chair*, *lamp*, *pain*, *stomach*, *fool*, *music*, *park*, *beef*, *stew*, *toast*, *spy*, *faith*, *bar*, *jail*, *tax*, and *fry* that hardly feel "foreign" to us now.
   3. *Latin*. The "Latinate" layer, most perceptible to us as a word class apart, came after the withdrawal of the French, with the increasing use of English as a language of learning—hence, *client*, *legal*, *scene*, *intellect*, *recipe*, *pulpit*, *exclude*, *necessary*, *tolerance*, *interest*, et alia.

E. Thus, an English that had developed without these lexical invasions would be incomprehensible and peculiar to us. For this reason, Icelanders can read literature in their language from the 1300s and Hebrew speakers can tackle Biblical Hebrew, but *Beowulf* is opaque to us.

F. Advantages and disadvantages.
   1. *Advantage*. Because English is so larded with Latin and French words, we have a good head start on learning the vocabularies of French and other languages descended from Latin. This is especially true of the more formal layers of these languages, because most of our words from French and Latin entered "from above," contributed by rulers and scientists. *Association*, *opportunité*, and *présent* give us little trouble.

2. *Disadvantage.* Because so little of the Old English rootstock remains in English, there is no other language that is close enough to ours to be especially easy to learn, as Portuguese is for Spaniards, Zulu is for Xhosa speakers, and so on. Thus, if a language does not have the Latinate inheritance that Western European languages do, then we must learn both its humble and its formal vocabulary from the ground up. Russian's "bread," "water," and "fish" are *xleb*, *voda*, and *ryba*; its "association," "opportunity," and "the present" are *soedinenje, vozmožnost*, and *nastojaščee*.

II. Word sharing is ordinary and inevitable.
   A. It is often supposed that this heavy borrowing makes English an especially "flexible" language. But all languages borrow words, usually a lot of them. Cultural disposition makes some languages more resistant to borrowing words than others, but the space to maneuver is pretty narrow.
   B. *"Real" languages as well as written ones.* For example, this borrowing does not require writing or extensive travel. In Australia, it is difficult to trace a family tree among the 260 languages originally spoken there because many have borrowed as much as 50 percent or more of their vocabularies from other Australian languages. This is partly because of widespread intermarriage.
   C. *Japanese.* Japan was traditionally one of the most isolated modern cultures in the world, but over the past few decades it has inhaled countless American English words, such as *beisuboru* ("baseball"), *T-shatsu* ("T-shirt"), *sukii* ("ski"), *fakkusu* ("fax:"), and *bouifurendo* ("boyfriend").
   D. *High and low.* Norman French left many diglossic doublets in English, such as *pig* and *pork* and *help* and *aid*. This is common across languages.
      1. *Japanese.* Japanese has thousands of Chinese-derived words, including the numbers one through four, *ichi*, *ni*, *san*, *shi*. The original Japanese numbers—*hitotsu*, *futatsu*, *mittsu*, *yottsu*—are used less, for example when giving children's ages.

2. *Vietnamese.* The Chinese occupied Vietnam for more than a thousand years, and Vietnamese is about 30 percent Chinese in its vocabulary, including doublets such as the written *hoả-xa* for "train" and the spoken native *xe lửa* meaning "train" in casual speech.

III. Word sharing and dialects: Dialects generally borrow from dialects.

A. *Doublets.* This means that a language may get two words from one, borrowing different versions of it from two dialects. *Chant* was borrowed from standard French's verb *chanter*, "to sing." But *cant*, in the sense of platitudinous talk, was borrowed from Norman French's version of the same verb, *canter*.

B. *Different dialects, different borrowings.* Scots English took on some Dutch words that dialects to the south did not. Thus, Standard English has such words as *cruise* and *easel*, but Scots has such words as *callan*, "lad," and *cowk*, "to retch." Because the Norse-speaking Viking invaders settled in what became Scotland, Scots also has a stronger Norse imprint than Standard English, such as *til* for "to," *gie* for "give," and *richt* for "right."

Thus, it is ordinary for languages to share words, and far beyond the level of obvious exoticisms, such as *sushi* and *taco*. Often, the borrowings help to trace the movement of peoples and the history of their languages.

IV. Word mixture in real life: Although it is easy to accept word mixture that happened in times long past, when we see it happening in our lifetimes, it often occasions discomfort, out of a sense that purity is compromised. But we are simply watching a time-honored process taking place.

A. *Spanglish.* When a Latino immigrant in the United States says *brecas* for "brakes," instead of the original Spanish *frenos*; or *carpeta* to refer to a rug rather than, as in original Spanish, a folder; or *Voy a manejar mi troca a la marketa* for "I'm going to drive my truck to the market," instead of *Voy a manejar mi camión al mercado*, speakers of Spanish in Spain, Mexico, and other Latin countries often see this as "polluted" Spanish. But this is as natural, and inevitable, a process as the influx of French words into English under the Norman occupation.

B. *English in the days of yore.* When the new French words were still processable as "new," there were even English speakers who decried them as "wrong." Man of letters John Cheke instructed in 1561 that "Our own tung shold be written cleane and pure, vnmixt and vnmangeled with borrowing of other tunges," following this with substituting *mooned* for *lunatic* and similar usages. (Interesting that both *pure* and *mangled* came from French!)

Essential Reading:

Bryson, Bill. *The Mother Tongue: English and How It Got That Way.* New York: William Morrow and Co., 1990.

Crystal, David. *The Cambridge Encyclopedia of the English Language.* Cambridge: Cambridge University Press, 1995.

Stavans, Ilan. *Spanglish: The Making of a New American Language.* New York: HarperCollins, 2003.

Questions to Consider:

1. Choose a sentence or two from a magazine or newspaper, look up the etymology of each word, and see how mixed English's vocabulary is. How does this make you feel about issues of language purity?
2. If you were an official in a foreign country whose language was taking in a great many words from English, would you advise that native words be constructed to substitute for the English ones, as the French Academy does? Or would you simply allow the influx of English words? How would you defend your position in either case?

Lecture Twenty-One
Language Mixture—Grammar

Scope: Languages also mix their grammars. Yiddish is basically a dialect of German, but it has not only many words but even grammatical features from Slavic languages, such as Polish. Indian Indo-European languages, such as Hindi, place their verbs at the end of sentences because the other language family of India has the same feature. In some cases, languages mix so intimately that they become new ones, such as Media Lengua in Ecuador, which uses Spanish words with endings and word order from the local Indian language Quechua. There are no languages without at least some signs of grammar mixture.

Outline

I. Introduction.

    A. Words are only the beginning of how languages mix. Languages consist not only of words but of how the words are put together: grammar. In situations where large numbers of people are bilingual, the two languages they speak often come to resemble one another on the level of sounds and sentence structure, as well as exchanging words—rather like married couples who gradually begin to look like each other over the decades.

    B. This happens most readily when literacy in the language is not widespread, such that there is relatively little sense that a standard variety is "The Language." For that reason, this kind of grammar mixture has largely occurred beneath the radar screen of writing—before the last several centuries in languages familiar to most of us. Yet its impact has played a major part in determining what the world's languages are like today, especially considering that only about 200 of the world's 6,000 languages are written regularly.

II. Basic examples.

    A. *Clicks in Khoi-San and Bantu.* The Khoi-San ("Bushman") languages of southern Africa are not the world's only languages with clicks. For example, some Bantu languages spoken near them have clicks: Miriam Makeba even made the clicks famous in a popular song in her native Xhosa. These Bantu languages inherited the clicks from Khoi-San languages long ago.

B. *Indo-Aryan languages.* We saw that Indo-European languages in India, such as Hindi, place the verb last in a sentence.

Hindi:

Mẽ	Apu	se	mila	tha.
I	Apu	with	meet	did

"I met Apu."

This is not an accident. Indo-European languages of Europe usually do not place their verbs at the end of the sentence or only do so optionally. Indian Indo-European languages borrowed this word order from languages of another family originally spoken in India, the Dravidian family. Below is a sentence in one of the main Dravidian languages, Kannada:

Kannada:

Avanu	nanage	bisketannu	tinisidanu.
He	to-me	biscuit	fed

"He fed me a biscuit."

C. Among linguists, it has always been known that languages regularly exchange words, but until rather recently, grammar mixture has often been treated as marginal, with basic processes of independent change seen as "basic." But it is increasingly clear that all of the languages of the world bear marks from both the words and the grammars of languages spoken close by.

III. Intertwined languages.

A. There are many languages in the world that are so mixed that they cannot be treated as either Language A or Language B; these are hybrids, in the same way that mules are neither horses nor donkeys.

B. Code-switching.
1. These languages begin with an ordinary process called *code-switching*, where speakers regularly alternate between one language and another, often within the same sentence.

2. *Nuyorican*. Here is an example of a Puerto Rican code-switching between Spanish and English in New York:

Why make Carol *sentarse atras*   *para que* everybody
                      ait   in back so that

has to move *para que*   *se salga*?
              so that   she gets out

Code-switching is common among bilinguals worldwide. Generally, code-switchers are fully competent in both languages but switch back and forth according to topic or when a word they are more familiar with in one language comes along and sparks a switch into that word's language.

C. *Media Lengua*. In some cases, code-switching becomes so well entrenched that a new language emerges, splitting the difference between the two languages. For example, among men in Ecuador who grew up speaking Quechua but spent long periods working in the capital Quito using Spanish, a new hybrid language called *Media Lengua*—"middle language"—emerged. Media Lengua uses Spanish words with the endings and word order of Quechua:

"I come to ask a favor."

Spanish:

Vengo para pedir un favor.
I-come for   ask   a   favor

Quechua:

Shuk fabur-da maña-nga-bu shamu-xu-ni.
one   favor   ask   come-ing-I

Media Lengua:

Unu **fabur**-ta **pidi**-nga-bu **bini**-xu-ni.
a   favor   ask   come-ing-I

Media Lengua uses the Spanish words but with the sound system of Quechua (Quechua does not have *e* or *o*) and with its endings and its word order, where the object (here, *favor*) comes before the verb.

D. *Mednyj Aleut*. In the 1800s, Russian traders colonized the Aleut Islands off Alaska and brought Aleuts (Eskimos) to work along with them on one of the islands (Copper Island). The traders and Aleut women produced children who created a language of their own, mixing, of all things, Russian with an Eskimo language.

Languages like this are not just random mixing on the spur of the moment. Mednyj Aleut has rules. Certain verb endings, such as the one in the sentence that follows, are from Russian, as are certain pronouns. Case endings on nouns as well as nouns and verbs themselves are usually from Aleut.

Mednyj Aleut:

Ya	tibe	cíbux	ukaɣla:ɣa:sa:l
I	**to you**	**package**	**bring-ed**

"I brought you a package."

E. There are intertwined languages mixing Russian and the Aleut language of Eskimos, English and the Gypsy language Romani, and many others.

IV. Biological analogies.

A. I have analogized language mixture to the mating of a horse and a mule, but this implies that language mixture is exceptional and that its results are somehow deficient. But another biological analogy is more appropriate. Lynn Margulis and other biologists have called attention to the fact that symbiosis—communal, co-dependent living between different species—is central to the existence of life as we know it. Plants derive crucial nutrients via the fungi in their roots that process nitrogen for them; cows could not digest their food without the bacteria filling their stomachs; and even the organelles within cells, such as mitochondria in animals, began as independent bacteria.

B. As Margulis has it:

In reality the tree of life often grows in on itself. Species come together, fuse, and make new beings, who start again. Biologists call the coming together of branches—whether blood vessels, roots, or fungal threads—anastomosis…. Anastomosis, although less frequent, is as important as branching. Symbiosis, like sex, brings previously evolved beings together into new partnerships. (Margulis, Lynn. *Symbiotic Planet: A New View of Evolution*. New York: Basic Books, 1998, p. 52.)

In broad view, the world's languages comprise tens of thousands of dialects harboring evidence of symbiotic matings in the past. Margulis describes anastomosis as "branches forming nets," and this analogy is so useful that it can replace the one of the flowering bush.

Essential Reading:

McWhorter, John H. *The Power of Babel*. New York: HarperCollins, 2001 (chapter 3).

Supplementary Reading:

Thomason, Sarah Grey. *Language Contact: An Introduction*. Washington, DC: Georgetown University Press, 2001.

Questions to Consider:

1. When you are learning a foreign language, it is natural to occasionally put things in ways that reflect your native language: in Spanish, *I like the book* is "to-me pleases the book": *Me gusta el libro*. But you would be less likely to say *ojo médico* for *eye doctor*. Can you think of reasons why some mistakes like this are more likely than others?

2. Although it is quite common for people to mix two languages when speaking, as code-switchers do, it is much less common for one person to speak in one language and the other to answer in another, even if both people speak both languages. (Only small immigrant children tend to do this as they begin switching from their home language to the national one.) Can you speculate about why adults are so reluctant to do this?

Lecture Twenty-Two
Language Mixture—Language Areas

Scope: When unrelated or distantly related languages are spoken in the same area for long periods, they tend to become more grammatically similar, because of widespread bilingualism. The classic case is Indo-European languages of the Balkans, which share various traits that they did not have originally. But linguists are discovering the same phenomenon across the world: languages of Southeast Asia stem from four different families but share a similar "template." Linguists are finding that the usual situation is that few new languages emerge, but the ones that exist stew together in this way; only invasions and migrations interrupt this process and create brand-new languages.

Outline

I. Grammar sharing does not occur only between pairs of languages.

    A. Not only do we see distinct languages with aspects of grammar that one must have borrowed from the other, but even distinct language groups or families that are so similar to one another in structure that it is clear that over time, a certain complex of grammatical traits has been shared and distributed widely, creating what is called a *language area*.

    B. Thus, in a language area, although it can appear that all the languages trace back to a single ancestor, in fact, they may trace to several different proto-languages. Their similarity has arisen over time from grammar mixture.

II. The Balkans.

    A. A classic example is the Indo-European languages in the Balkans. Romanian is a Romance language. Albanian is a highly distinct branch of its own, as is Greek. Serbo-Croatian, Macedonian, and Bulgarian are Slavic languages.

    B. Yet these languages share several grammatical patterns that were not initially present in most of the languages when they emerged. For example, Romance languages usually place the definite article before the noun (Spanish: *el hombre*, Italian: *il uomo*), but Romanian places its definite article after the noun: *om-**ul***.

C. This placement is the result of the development of Romanian in an area where there was once a great deal of bilingualism, partly because of migrations and invasions. Some of the languages placed their definite article after the noun. Bulgarian for "the woman" is *žena-**ta***; Albanian for "the friend" is *mik-**u***. This is why Romanian for "the man" is *om-ul*.

D. Then, it is odd that Bulgarian has a definite article at all because Slavic languages usually do not (Russian has no words for *the* or *a*). Bulgarian inherited this characteristic from such languages as Romanian and Albanian.

E. This is called a *Sprachbund*—a group of languages that have become increasingly similar to one another over time because of heavy bi- or multilingualism.

III. The "Sinosphere."

A. Southeastern Asia contains several distinct language families. The southern Chinese varieties, such as Cantonese, belong to the *Sino-Tibetan* family. Thai and Laotian are members of a different family called *Tai-Kadai*. Vietnamese and Cambodian are members of yet another family, *Austroasiatic*, and there are also scattered small languages, such as Hmong, part of a family called *Miao-Yao*.

B. Yet all these languages are based on a common "game plan." We saw some of it in Cantonese in Lecture Ten, with its particles at the end of sentences that convey attitude and its classifiers used with numbers, such as our *two head of cattle* instead of *two cattle*. But there are many other features typical across these families. A language of this area tends to be tonal, to have no gender marking or case marking, to have most words consist of a single syllable instead of two or more, and so on.

C. This phenomenon can be partly explained by the fact that Chinese speakers conquered and migrated southward, lending parts of their grammar to the languages they encountered. But the process went both ways: Chinese in the south became more like the languages it encountered, as well.

D. As a result, on first glance, Cantonese, Vietnamese, Thai, and Hmong appear to trace to a common ancestor, being so unlike other language families and so similar to one another. But actually, the resemblance is due to millennia of constant grammar sharing. Linguist James Matisoff has termed this language area a "Sinosphere."

IV. The European language area.

    A. Even Western Europe is a language area, although when we speak a European language and are most exposed to others, it is easy to suppose that European features are simply "normal."

    B. *Articles*. For example, as normal as it seems to us for a language to have words for *a* and *the*, in fact, only about one in five of the world's languages do, with many having neither (such as the ones in the Sinosphere). Proto-Indo-European did not have words for *a* and *the*. Instead, these words developed in a great many of its children and ones of different subfamilies spoken in the same region. In addition, even Hungarian has *a* and *the*, despite being of a different family altogether, Uralic, which elsewhere tends not to have articles. The prevalence of this feature in Western Europe is due to grammar sharing over time, between subfamilies and even families of language.

    C. Another example is the *perfect* construction with *have*. To express the perfect with *have* in a sentence such as *I have sewn this dress* is almost exclusively found in Europe. Again, this was not a feature of Proto-Indo-European, yet as rare as it is in languages of the world, it has developed again and again in various of its descendants.

    D. These are a few of many ways in which European languages are similar, even though Proto-Indo-European lacked the feature and the feature often appears in languages outside of Indo-European, including Finnish, Hungarian, or Basque.

V. Equilibrium and punctuation.

    A. The linguist R. M. W. Dixon has argued influentially that the development of language areas is a norm. The typical situation worldwide has been that groups of languages spoken by small numbers of people have coexisted for millennia, sharing words and grammar and becoming increasingly alike. This situation is one of what Dixon terms *linguistic equilibrium*, in which it is rare that new languages develop.

B. However, invasions, migrations, and geographical upheavals sometimes lead speakers of a language to move to other regions, replacing the languages of previous inhabitants. The new groups of speakers, separated from the original ones, develop new branches of the original language in each new location. Dixon terms this *punctuation*, modeled on the evolutionary theory of paleontologists Niles Eldredge and Stephen Jay Gould that evolution proceeds in abrupt leaps rather than tiny steps. Under Dixon's theory, the branching of a language into new ones is a special circumstance, a leaping kind of change distinct from the relative stasis of an equilibrium situation.

Essential Reading:

Dixon, R. M. W. *The Rise and Fall of Languages*. Cambridge: Cambridge University Press, 1997.

Questions to Consider:

1. Taking classes in European languages, such as French, Spanish, and German, can make it seem as if languages only vary so much from English in terms of grammar: master some endings and get used to gender marking and the rest is relatively straightforward. But increasingly, Americans are learning languages from further away, such as Chinese, Japanese, and Arabic. If you have approached one of these, what were some of the differences in how they were put together, showing that there is a rough "European" game plan that most languages are *not* based on?

2. As linguists realize how much languages have shared grammars over the years, it is becoming increasingly clear that the comparative reconstruction method will be of little use in tracing back to proto-languages for many of the world's language families. In your opinion, does this suggest that the enterprise should be given up, or does it perhaps make the methods of the Proto-World school more attractive?

Lecture Twenty-Three
Language Develops Beyond the Call of Duty

Scope: A great deal of a language's grammar is a kind of overgrowth, marking nuances of life that many or most languages do without. Some languages require one to mark how one learned whatever one is saying; others mark possession differently, according to whether one refers to an object or a body part. Even the gender marking familiar from European languages is a frill, absent in thousands of languages. The theme is decoration over necessity.

Outline

I. Introduction.

  A. A central aspect of how languages and dialects develop through time is that all of them are replete with features that, in the strict sense, they do not need. This is important to realize not only for the sheer wonder of it, but also because an awareness of it sheds insight on how languages' structure is determined in part by their history, which we will explore in later lectures.

  B. For example, the *have*-perfect is not only rare across languages but unnecessary. The perfect merely implies that something that happened in the past is still relevant in the present, and a great many languages leave that semantic shade to context. When Dorn at the end of Chekhov's *The Seagull* says, "Konstantin Gavrilovich has shot himself," in Russian, it simply translates as "Konstantin Gavrilovich shot himself"—that the event has ongoing implications is quite clear from context.

II. Evidential markers.

  A. In many languages, when one states something, one must also indicate how one learned the statement, through seeing, hearing, general sense, or the like. In English, we can say *I saw that they are tearing down the building*, but it is quite proper to just say *They are tearing down the building*. In many languages, such a sentence would be as incomplete as *They tearing down building* would be to us.

B. Tuyuca is spoken in the Amazon and has several such markers: Evidential markers in Tuyuca:

Kiti-gï tii   -gí   "He is chopping trees" (I hear him)

               -í   "He is chopping trees" (I see him)

               -hɔ̀i   "Apparently he is chopping trees" (I can't tell)

               -yigï   "They say he chopped trees"

chop trees-he AUX

C. The way these markers develop is through the grammaticalization that we examined in Lecture Four. For example, in the North American Native American language Makah, to say that from what one sees, the weather is bad, one says, "it's bad weather," then a suffix is added, meaning that the statement is based on seeing something, *-pid*. The *-pid* started out as a separate verb meaning "it is seen" but eroded and grammaticalized into becoming an evidential marker.

Makah:

wikicaxak-**pid**
"It's bad weather—from what it looks like." ("Looks like bad weather.")

D. Importantly, evidential markers like this are not necessary. In all languages, one might specify how one learned something, but it is a frill to have to indicate it as an obligation. Grammaticalization has a way of taking a ball and running with it: what begins as an indication of something concrete and necessary often devolves into a useless habit.

III. Alienable possession.

A. One *has* one's ear in a different way than one *has* a table, and *has* one's relative in a different way than one *has* a car. In English, we use the same word *have* for both conceptions, but just as often, languages mark this subtle difference.

B. In Mandinka in West Africa, for example, to say "your father," one says *i faamaa*, but to say "your well," one says *i la koloŋo*. The *la* particle signals that something is possessed in the "table" way instead of the "ear" way. Linguists differentiate these concepts as *alienable possession* (the table kind) and *inalienable possession* (the ear kind).

Mandinka

i faamaa "your father"

i la koloŋo "your well"

IV. Inherent reflexive marking.

A. To avoid a sense that this is just a trait of exotic languages, we return to a European frill of this kind. In English, one can say *I wash myself*—this is normal *reflexivity*, marking an action that one performs upon oneself. But in other European languages, one pays much closer attention to whether an action occurs upon oneself. In Spanish, *yo **me** siento* means "I sit myself down." In French, *je **me** fâche* is "I anger myself"; in German, *ich erinnere **mich*** is "I remember myself."

B. Here, the literal kind of reflexivity that English has went a step further. Now, the reflexive marker is grammaticalized as a way of indicating even the slightest degree to which one could conceive of an action as happening to a person rather than being effected by the person on something or someone else.

V. Gender marking.

A. In European and many other languages, nouns are divided into gender classes. Spanish has masculine and feminine, marked with an article and often with the final vowel: ***el** sombrero*, ***la** casa*. German has three: "the spoon," "the fork," and "the knife" are ***der** Löffel*, ***die** Gabel*, and ***das** Messer*. This is not necessary in a language: it is an accident of history.

B. *Stage one*. In many languages, we can see how this marking begins. In Dyirbal, spoken in Australia, all nouns must be preceded by a separate word. Which word a noun takes depends on which of four categories it fits into. One is for males and animals, another for female things, another for food that is not flesh, and another is the grab bag.

Dyirbal gender classifiers:

	MARKER	EXAMPLE
masculine, animals	bayi	bayi yaṛa "man"
feminine	balan	balan gabay "girl"
nonflesh food	balam	balam gayga "cake"
grab bag	bala	bala yugu "wood"

- **C.** *Stage two.* Over time, separate words such as these erode and become prefixes or suffixes—grammaticalization again. At first, the new prefixes or suffixes still correspond fairly well to categories. Swahili is at this stage. Swahili has seven "genders" (although because sex is not one of the categories marked, linguists call them *noun classes*). The one with an *m-* prefix contains people: ***m****tu*, "man"; ***m****toto*, "child." The one with an *n-* prefix contains animals: ***n****dege*, "bird"; ***n****zige*, "locust."

- **D.** *Stage three.* But as time goes on, sound change, cultural changes, eccentric semantic switches (such as the one that made the word for *sister-in-law* masculine in Proto-Indo-European), and other processes make the correspondence between marker and category increasingly vague. European languages are an example of this stage, where only marking actual male beings masculine and actual female beings feminine makes any immediate sense anymore.

VI. Thus, a great deal of what a language's grammar pays attention to is technically a kind of window dressing. Keep in mind that there are actually some languages that do not mark tense at all, and some where *I* and *we* are the same word, *he* and *they* are the same word, and so on, because pronouns mark person but not number! This shows that it is inherent to human language to overelaborate.

Essential Reading:

McWhorter, John H. *The Power of Babel.* New York: HarperCollins, 2001 (chapter 5).

Questions to Consider:

1. To people speaking languages with alienable possessive marking, English appears rather crude in making no distinction between *my mother* and *my chair*. Then to us, a language that cannot distinguish *Elvis left the building* from *Elvis has left the building* seems somehow

impoverished. Think of some meanings that a foreign language you are familiar with marks that English doesn't and some distinctions English marks that the foreign language does not.

2. Often, languages differ not in simply whether they express a concept or not, but in how obligatory it is to express the concept. English, for example, does not have obligatory evidential marking, as Tuyuca does, but we do express such things if necessary. Think of some words, expressions, or even intonations English uses to indicate sources of information.

Lecture Twenty-Four
Language Interrupted

Scope: Generally, a language spoken by a small, isolated group will be much more complicated than English. In fact, it is typical for languages to be vastly overgrown in this way. Languages are "streamlined" when history leads them to be learned more as second languages than as first ones, which abbreviates some of the more difficult parts of their grammars. This means that a language such as Tsez of the Caucasus Mountains in Asia is so complex that one wonders how it could be learned, while one variety of Indonesian created by adult speakers of local languages is so streamlined that one wonders how it conveys enough meaning to be useful! Such languages as English and Mandarin Chinese are intermediate cases.

Outline

I. Introduction.

    A. Now that we have seen that languages tend naturally to develop beyond what is necessary to communication, we are in a position to begin examining how languages' complexity can differ depending on historical circumstance.

    B. One lesson I have tried to convey is that there are no "simple" languages in the world, even when they do not have tables of endings as European languages tend to. A language without endings will usually have tones like Chinese. Overall, there are many ways for a language to be complex beyond even tones, such as the classifiers, evidential markers, distinctions between shades of possession, and other features we have seen in these lectures.

    C. Linguists often remind students and readers that all languages are complex, with the implication that all languages are equally complex. This, however, is not quite true. In reality, many languages are more complex than others.

    D. It is natural to suppose that the more advanced a society is, the more complex its language will be. And it is true that only a language with a history of writing can amass an enormous vocabulary. But a language is not only its words but also its grammar, and usually, a language spoken by a small, preliterate group is more complicated than English, Spanish, Japanese, or other First World languages.

II. How complex can languages get? The case of Tsez.

   A. Tsez is spoken in the Caucasus Mountains in Asia by about 14,000 people. It does not have a large written literature: it is mostly a spoken language.

   B. In Tsez, there are four "genders" of noun. There is a masculine class and a feminine one. But the feminine gender also contains objects that are flat or pointed (go figure). Another gender has many animals but also lots of other things, and the fourth one has various other inanimate objects.

   C. The gender marker is not attached to the noun but to the verbs, adjectives, adverbs, or prepositions associated with the noun. Here, for example, we see three of the gender markers on verbs following the noun.

   eniy **y**-ˁuλ'-no "the mother feared"

   buq **b**-ajnosi "the sun rose"

   tatanu ɣudi **r**-oqxo "the day warmed up"

   D. But then, there is a bizarre wrinkle—the gender markers are only used when the word begins with a vowel! If it begins with a consonant there is no marker. This means that, in a way, the exception is the rule:

   kid **y**-iys "the girl knows"

   kid __-božizi yoq-xo "the girl believes"

   E. Tsez also has many case markers, like Latin. But these are often extremely irregular, as if such differences as *children* versus *child* and *people* versus *person* were typical of hundreds of nouns in English. The word for *fish* is regular, but look what happens when the same endings are added to the words for *tongue* and *water*.

These things must simply be learned by rote:

besuro "fish"	giri "tongue"	ɬi "water"
besuro-**s** "the fish's"	giri-**mos** "the tongue's"	ɬ-**ās** "water's"
besuro-**bi** "fishes" (fish)	giri-**mabi** "tongues"	ɬ-**idabi** "waters"

F. In addition, Tsez has a trait common in small languages: a subject takes an ending when it has an object but not when it doesn't. Therefore, to say *The girl knows* is one thing, but to say *The girl washed the dress* means putting a special ending onto the word for *girl*! This is called *ergativity*.

Kid y-iys
"the girl knows"

kid-**ba**   ged   esay-si.
"girl-ERG   dress   washed"

"The girl washed the dress."

G. Finally, Tsez is full of unusual sounds, many made back in the throat, with fine variations on these to boot, including mixtures of them.

H. And of course, there are, as in all languages, exceptions galore to the rules, plus all kinds of other complications (for example, Tsez has evidential marking). Yet people speak this language without effort every day. This is what "real" languages are like. We find similarly complex grammars in languages spoken by small tribes in the Amazon and many other locations. It has been said that Native American languages, such as Cree and Ojibwa, are so complex that children are not fully competent in them until the age of 10.

III. How simple can languages get? The case of Riau Indonesian.

A. A contrasting case is a dialect of Indonesian spoken in Sumatra, called Riau Indonesian. Standard Indonesian appears "normally" complex to the English speaker, with a certain number of prefixes and endings, a set word order, and so on. But while Tsez makes one wonder how people could speak it without having a stroke, Riau Indonesian makes one wonder how one could speak it and even be understood.

B. This is a dialect spoken by human beings every day that has no endings, no tones, no articles, and no word order at all. Sentences are only placed in time if context alone does not make it clear, and even then, only with such words as *already* and *tomorrow*, not with special endings or words used only to mark tense. There is no verb "to be." The same word means *he*, *she*, *it*, and *they*.

C. This means that a sentence in Riau Indonesian can have endless meanings according to context. For example, *ayam* means *chicken* and *makan* means *eat*. The sentence *ayam makan* can mean, "The chicken is eating," "The chicken ate," "The chicken will eat," "The chicken is being eaten," "The chicken is making somebody eat," "Somebody is eating for the chicken," "The chicken that is eating," "Where the chicken is eating," "When the chicken is eating," "How the chicken is eating," and so on.

D. But this simplicity is not connected to the fact that its speakers are not First Worlders. Riau Indonesian developed among people who spoke various languages related to Indonesian in Sumatra as first languages and learned Indonesian as a second one. Their first languages are "typical" in complexity, with very complex prefixes, and so on. But as is common among adults, when these people learned Indonesian as a second language, they did not acquire it completely. This is especially common when people learn a language outside of the school setting. Children born into a society where most people are speaking a language incompletely learn that variety and pass it down the generations.

IV. An intermediate case: Mandarin Chinese.

A. It is common worldwide for a language to be streamlined somewhat when at one point, more people learn it as a second language than as a first one. Languages like this are less imposingly complex than a language such as Tsez.

B. This is true of Mandarin Chinese in comparison to other Chinese languages, such as Cantonese. Mandarin has four tones; Cantonese has six (or depending on how one counts, nine). A Mandarin word can end only in *n* or "ng"—there is no such word in Mandarin as *fap* or *fam*. But a Cantonese word can end in six different consonants, *p*, *t*, *k*, *m*, *n*, and "ng." Cantonese has about 30 of the sentence-final particles that convey attitude; Mandarin has only about a half dozen of these. Mandarin is the "easy" language among the Chinese group.

C. In antiquity, the northern part of China where Mandarin is spoken was ruled by people speaking such languages as Mongolian and Manchu. These people learned Mandarin as a second language and passed this "learner's variety" down the generations. Chinese developed "normally" in the south and became such varieties as Cantonese and Taiwanese. In the north, Chinese was, as it were, "semi-Riau-ized."

V. Other cases: Many languages have undergone what Mandarin did. Swahili is one of the only Bantu languages out of more than 500 that has no tones, and this is because only a small number of Muslim people on the east African coast use it as a first language. For centuries, Swahili has been east Africa's main lingua franca, learned by most of its speakers as a second or third language. This has rendered it less Tsez-esque than the other Bantu languages.

VI. Our lesson is that it is normal for languages to be awesomely complex, regardless of the societal level of advancement of their speakers. What is unusual is when languages are less complex than these tribal ones. Languages get "shaved down" when history leads them to be spoken more as second languages than as first ones. We are now in a position to understand some aspects of English better, then to proceed to pidgin and creole languages.

Essential Reading:
McWhorter, John H. *The Power of Babel*. New York: HarperCollins, 2001 (chapter 5).

Questions to Consider:
1. If languages tend to be more complex in smaller, isolated societies, then this suggests that the languages that are spreading to millions of people scattered across vast areas will be increasingly simple in their structure. Is this a good thing or a bad one?

2. Compared to its close relatives, such as German and Swedish, English is rather streamlined: for example, in the present tense, it has but one ending, third person singular -*s*. Some linguists have supposed that this was just an accident, but what alternative analysis might this trait of English suggest?

Lecture Twenty-Five
A New Perspective on the Story of English

Scope: The preceding lectures allow us to see the history of English in a new light. English is, basically, one of today's branches of Proto-Indo-European. The Germanic family that English belongs to was distinguished by odd consonant changes, changes in stress that encouraged endings to wear off, and possibly, an ancient encounter with a Semitic language, leaving words that do not trace to Indo-European at all. Then the branch of Germanic that the Angles, Saxons, and Jutes brought to England came to be learned as much by Viking invaders as by natives, which streamlined English into the one Germanic language without such distinctions as *here* and *hither* and the one Indo-European language of Europe with no gender markers.

Outline

I. Introduction.
   A. Generally, the story of English is told as beginning with the arrival of the Angles, Jutes, and Saxons from continental Europe, followed by their language incorporating vocabulary from the original Celtic inhabitants, then the Scandinavian Vikings, then the Normans, and then Latin, Greek, and other languages.
   B. But what we have seen so far in these lectures allows us to see how English began and why it is the way it is today from new perspectives.

II. Proto-Indo-European.
   A. English, like all languages, is the product of change from a former language: that is, English is one step along a path of continuous development. The furthest back we can trace English, then, is Proto-Indo-European.
   B. At this stage, "English" is barely perceptible. Here is a piece of a folk tale constructed in the Proto-Indo-European of about 2500 B.C. (hypothetically, of course):

Tod	kekluwōs,	owis	agrom	ebhuget.
that	hearing	sheep	field	fled

"On hearing that, the sheep ran off into the plain."

The word *tod* eventually did become *that*, and believe it or not, *kekluwōs* was a form of the verb that did eventually become *hear*. But *field* traces back to a Proto-Indo-European root meaning "to fill," and *flee* to one meaning "flow"—these words are products of the semantic change we saw in Lecture Five.

III. The Germanic subfamily.

   A. The next step to English is Germanic, one of the many branches that Proto-Indo-European developed as its speakers moved into Europe and eastward into Asia. Germanic is thought to have emerged in southern Scandinavia or in Denmark and around the Elbe River in about 1000 B.C. The Germanic proto-language was English's next closest ancestor after Proto-Indo-European.

   B. *Erosion of endings*. In this language, stress in words tended to drift to the first syllable. This left the final sounds in words highly unstressed, vulnerable to wearing away. Because of this, Proto-Germanic did not have as many endings on nouns and verbs as many other Indo-European languages had. Recall Lithuanian's seven cases: Proto-Germanic had just four. This set the scene for how few case marking suffixes English has.

   C. *Semitic vocabulary?*

   1. Proto-Germanic was also odd in that one in three Germanic words do not trace to Proto-Indo-European (*sheep* is one of them). This suggests that a group of speakers of some other language learned a branch of Proto-Indo-European and lent it many of their original words.

   2. Recall Grimm's Law from Lecture Eight, where Proto-Indo-European *p* changed to *f*, *d* to *t*, and so on, only in Germanic. This is a very odd kind of change, which suggests that it was the result of speakers of a language with a very different sound system than Proto-Indo-European's.

   3. But what would the language have been? Linguist Theo Vennemann thinks it was a Semitic language, given that

Semitic-speaking sailors traveled the European coast far back in antiquity. The word *maiden*, cognate to German *Mädchen*, traces back to a Proto-Germanic word **maghatis*. The reconstructed Proto-Semitic word for girl is **maḥat*. In Germanic, a verb often marks past tense with a change of vowel instead of adding -*ed*, such as s*i*nk, s*a*nk. Recall how Semitic words work from Lecture Ten, **kitāb**, "book"; **kātib**, "writer."

IV. Germanic in England.

    A. Proto-Germanic split into three branches, and some of the peoples who spoke the western one settled in England. (Their relatives today in the Netherlands speak Frisian and Dutch.) The language they developed, Anglo-Saxon or Old English, was one much like German.

    B. But it did not stay this way. Part of the reason was the massive influx of borrowed words that we saw in Lecture Twenty. But English also changed its grammar considerably. Today, English is not only the one Germanic language that has lost all gender marking but also the only Indo-European language of all Europe without it. English is the only Germanic language without the inherent reflexives from the last lecture: in German, one remembers oneself, one hurries oneself, but in English, one simply remembers and hurries. In Lecture Seven, I noted that English no longer makes any distinction between *here* and *hither*, *where* and *whither*, and so on. However, all of the other Germanic languages do. There are many other cases like this in English.

    C. English is, in this sense, somewhat simpler than German, Dutch, Swedish, and its other sister languages. English was learned as a second language more than as a first, then passed down in this fashion. Specifically, it was likely in the northern half of England after the Viking invasions at the end of the 8th century that English was streamlined in this way.

V. What is English? English, then, is a descendant of Proto-Indo-European that, along the way toward its emergence, lost most of its case endings and a third of its vocabulary. It replaced that vocabulary with words from a language possibly related to Arabic and Hebrew, then supplemented this with words from, most copiously, Old Norse, Norman French, Dutch, Latin, and Greek. Meanwhile, it was learned so much as a second language by Vikings that its grammar was restrained somewhat from the overgrowth typical of languages that develop uninterrupted. A lot can happen to a language in 4,500 years!

Essential Reading:

Comrie, Bernard, Stephen Matthews, and Maria Polinsky, eds. *The Atlas of Languages*. New York: Facts on File, 2003.

Supplementary Reading:

Baugh, A. C., and T. Cable. *A History of the English Language*. Englewood Cliffs, NJ: Prentice-Hall, 1978.

Questions to Consider:

1. As an imaginative exercise, take the English version of the folk tale passage from Section II.B. of this outline and, based on the language change processes we have seen throughout the series so far, project English forward 2,000 years. How might sounds change? Could we develop new prefixes or suffixes? Evidential markers? The sky's the limit.

2. Icelanders can read the version of their language from a thousand years ago with relative ease, but we can only do so after courses of training because English has changed so much. Do you think that this deprives English speakers of an immediately accessible historical literature and encourages cultural fragmentation, or do you embrace the bastard history of the language as a testament to the forces of hybridity over time?

Lecture Twenty-Six
Does Culture Drive Language Change?

Scope: Amateur linguist Benjamin Lee Whorf presented a hypothesis in the 1930s that features of our grammars channel how we think. This may encourage a sense that language structure and, by extension, change is driven significantly by culture rather than being an independently driven process. However, the Sapir-Whorf hypothesis was based on faulty evidence and is even counterintuitive. In experiments, it has been shown to be true only in small degrees, such as color perception. Language and culture are surely related, but not as intimately as some researchers would assume.

Outline

I. Introduction.

   A. Before proceeding, it is important that we address a hypothesis commonly taught and written about, which has deep implications for how we conceive of language change and how languages differ from one another.

   B. Starting in the 1930s, amateur linguist Benjamin Lee Whorf, building on insights originated by his mentor, linguist Edward Sapir, presented a hypothesis that our ways of processing the world are channeled by the structure of our language. This has been called the *Sapir-Whorf hypothesis*.

   C. Despite how widely this theory has been broadcast, the actual verdict on it has not been at all promising. Given the theory's implication that language and how it develops is determined in some significant way by culture, rather than by the faceless but fascinating processes of structural change, it is important that we get a closer look at this theory and its history.

II. Whorf's hypothesis.

   A. A signature quotation from Whorf is this one:

      We cut nature up, organize it into concepts, and ascribe significances as we do, largely because we are parties to an agreement to organize it in this way—an agreement that holds throughout our speech community and is codified in the patterns of our language. The agreement is, of course, an implicit and unstated one, BUT ITS TERMS ARE ABSOLUTELY OBLIGATORY; we cannot talk at all except by subscribing to the organization and classification of data which the agreement decrees." (Whorf, Benjamin Lee. *Language, Thought, and Reality: Selected Writings of Benjamin Lee Whorf*, edited by J. B. Carroll. Cambridge, MA: MIT Press, 1956, pp. 213–214.)

B. Whorf and Hopi.
    1. Whorf noted that the language of the Hopi Indians has a word, *masa'ytaka*, for all flying things except birds, while English requires separate words for all such things (*pilot*, *airplane*, *dragonfly*). Hopi has a word for water as it occurs in nature (*pāhe*) and a word for water as drunk and cooked with (*kēyi*); English has just *water* for both. He proposed that differences like this signal different ways of viewing the world.
    2. Whorf depicted Hopi as having no words or grammar placing actions in time similar to English's past and future markers. He claimed that this corresponded to the Hopi's having a cyclical, holistic sense of time in contrast to European language speakers' more linear one:

    Our objectified view of time is, however, favorable to historicity and to everything connected with the keeping of records, while the Hopi view is unfavorable thereto. The latter is too subtle, complex, and ever-developing, supplying no ready-made answer to the question of when "one" event ends and "another" begins. (Whorf, Benjamin Lee. *Language, Thought, and Reality: Selected Writings of Benjamin Lee Whorf*, edited by J. B. Carroll. Cambridge, MA: MIT Press, 1956, p. 153.)

    3. Part of Whorf's intention was to demonstrate that indigenous peoples are not "primitives." This was not as widely taught and known in his day as it is now, and thus, his portrait of Hopi language and thought is couched to show its superiority to ours:

    Does the Hopi language show here a higher plane of thinking, a more rational analysis of situations, than our vaunted English? Of course it does. In this field and in various others,

English compared to Hopi is like a bludgeon compared to a rapier. (Whorf, Benjamin Lee. *Language, Thought, and Reality: Selected Writings of Benjamin Lee Whorf*, edited by J. B. Carroll. Cambridge, MA: MIT Press, 1956, p. 85.)

4. Whorf added an important caveat, that the issue was less what we can think than what we think of most readily:

The important distinction between HABITUAL and POTENTIAL behavior enters here. The potential range of perception and thought is probably pretty much the same for all men. However, we would be immobilized if we tried to notice, report, and think of all possible discriminations in experience at each moment of our lives. Most of the time we rely on the discriminations to which our language is geared, on what Sapir termed "grooves of habitual expression." (Whorf, Benjamin Lee. *Language, Thought, and Reality: Selected Writings of Benjamin Lee Whorf*, edited by J. B. Carroll. Cambridge, MA: MIT Press, 1956, p. 117.)

III. Problems with the Sapir-Whorf hypothesis.

A. For one, Whorf's analysis of Hopi grammar was erroneous. Linguists have since shown that Hopi indeed has markers situating actions in time and that Hopi culture keeps careful time-based records with various calendars and sundials.

B. There are also intuitive problems with the hypothesis. We have seen that many languages mark the difference between how one has an eye versus how one has a chair. This would seem to index a focus in a culture on materialism. But this distinction is very rare in languages spoken by First World, capitalist nations and most common in languages spoken by indigenous peoples.

C. The idea that language channels thought is also less intuitive when applied to languages we are familiar with rather than exotic ones.

1. Western European languages tend to have two verbs for our *know*: one for being familiar with a person (that is, Spanish *conocer*, French *connaître*) and one for factual knowledge (that is, Spanish *saber*, French *savoir*). Yet do we sense that Europeans are more sensitive to the difference between knowing a person and knowing a fact than we are?

2. In English, *scissors*, *pants*, and *glasses* are marked with the plural. In Dutch, they are singular (*schaar*, *broek*, *bril*). But do we think of scissors as "two things"? Is a pair of pants "two things" to us?

D. Finally, to imply that language channels thought leads to uncomfortable implications given the difference between a language such as Tsez or European languages and ones like Riau Indonesian, where it often seems as if one barely needs to say much at all! Do Riau Indonesian speakers think less richly than shepherds in the Caucusus Mountains and functionaries in Brussels?

IV. Verdict from the experiments.

A. *Navajo and objects*. Navajo has different verbs for handling objects depending on their shape: *šańléh* for long, flexible objects, *šańṭį́h* for long, rigid ones, and so on. In an experiment, Navajo children tended to distinguish objects by shape and form rather than size and color, as English-speaking children did. However, in a later experiment, white middle-class children tended to distinguish by shape and form more than black children from Harlem, with social class being the overall predictor. Culture rather than language was the factor.

B. *Navajo and motion*. In another study, a researcher claimed that Navajo grammar marks subtler shades of motion than English and linked this to their traditional nomadism. But how exotic is it that Navajo has separate verbs for "move on all fours," "move at a run," "move by flying," "move by floating on water," and "move by rolling" when English has *crawl*, *run*, *fly*, *float*, and *roll*? Nothing in the experiment differed from verbs of motion in many other grammars spoken by sedentary people.

C. Only a few experiments have shown language channeling thought. For example, the Berinmo, hunter-gatherers of Papua New Guinea, have one term for what we distinguish as green and blue. In experiments, they distinguish green and blue more slowly than English speakers. However, they have two words for different shades of what English simply uses the one word *yellow* for. Given chips in a wide range of colors, they separate these two faster than English speakers.

D. But this and other experiments show only minor differences in sensitivity to color, material, and spatial orientation. There is no evidence of larger spiritual or cultural differences determined by grammar.

Essential Reading:

Pinker, Steven. *The Language Instinct*. New York: HarperCollins, 1994 (chapter 3).

Whorf, Benjamin Lee. *Language, Thought, and Reality: Selected Writings of Benjamin Lee Whorf*, edited by J. B. Carroll. Cambridge, MA: MIT Press, 1956.

Supplementary Reading:

Lucy, John A. *Language Diversity and Thought: A Reformulation of the Linguistic Relativity Hypothesis*. Cambridge: Cambridge University Press, 1992.

Questions to Consider:

1. The Sapir-Whorf hypothesis exerts an endless fascination on a great many—a professor can feel the hush in a classroom when lecturing on the subject. Why do you think the hypothesis is so stimulating to so many? Or, more specifically, why is it that so many spontaneously hope that the hypothesis is true?

2. French has gender marking: masculine, *le bateau*, "the boat"; feminine, *la table*, "the table." Recent experiments have shown that French speakers, asked to characterize how a table might talk, tend to suppose that it would be in a high, feminine voice and that their sense of inanimate objects' "voices" tends to correlate with gender. In your opinion, does this finding suggest that French creates a different way of viewing the world than English does, or does the finding strike you as largely incidental to "thought" per se?

Lecture Twenty-Seven
Language Starts Over—Pidgins

Scope: Many situations in the world create stripped-down versions of a language that are suitable for passing, utilitarian use. These are called *pidgins*, and they have a minimum of the frills that typify older languages. For example, in the 1700s and 1800s, Norwegian and Russian traders used a makeshift language, *Russenorsk*, with about 300 words borrowed partly from Russian and partly from Norwegian. Native Americans in North America once used an English pidgin of this kind. Although some older languages have less elaborate grammars than others, all have nuanced vocabulary and grammars complex enough to render sophisticated thought. Pidgins do not.

Outline

I. Introduction.

   A. Generally, languages both simplify and elaborate as they age, maintaining a high level of complexity at all times. When a language is learned as a second language more than as a first, its level of complexity drops, but it retains a considerable degree of unnecessary equipment.

   B. However, there are many contexts in the world where only partial command of a language is necessary. A great deal of communication can take place with just a few hundred words and an elementary grammar. This kind of speaking is called using a *pidgin* version of a language.

   C. The word comes from Chinese *pei tsin*, "pay money," which is what traders in Canton called the pidgin English they used there from the 1600s to the 1900s.

II. Typical example: Russenorsk.

   A. Starting in the late 1700s, Russian traders would spend summers in Norway trading timber for fish. The traders used a makeshift combination of Russian and Norwegian.

©2004 The Teaching Company.

B. One sentence was *Sobaku po moja skib*, which meant, "There is a dog on my ship."

Russenorsk:

Sobaku	po	moja	skib.
dog	on	my	ship

"There's a dog on my ship."

Sobaku is Russian for "dog"; *skib* is from Norwegian for "ship." *Moja* is Russian, and *po* is Norwegian, but *po* in Russian has a similar meaning. Speakers of the pidgin called it *moja po tvoja*, "me in yours."

C. As a pidgin, Russenorsk had no articles, no tense marking, no gender, no case markers, no verb conjugations. The vocabulary had only about 300 words. As a result, a single preposition, *po*, did the work of an army:

po moja stova	"at my house"
po Arkangel	"to Archangel"
po vater	"into the water"
po lan	"on land"

D. Pidgins are not real languages, nor are they quite the same as anyone's flailing attempt to render a language they barely know. Russenorsk was not completely word soup: there were loose rules. For example, there were many Norwegian or Russian prepositions that could have been used as an all-purpose one besides *po*: the use of *po* was a convention.

III. American Indian Pidgin English.

    A. Russenorsk split two languages fifty-fifty, but this is not the usual case. When Native Americans first encountered English, they usually retained their native languages and used English only when necessary, such as for trade. This is how pidgins typically arise, and as a result, an English pidgin was spoken by Indians across the continent.

B. It had some conventions, such as *heap* for "very" and *squaw* for "woman," which came from the Narragansett language of Rhode Island. Here is a sample:

American Indian Pidgin English:

You silly. You weak. You baby-hands. No catch horse. No kill buffalo. No good but for sit still—read book.

Look squaw in face—see him smile—which is all one he say yes!

C. Notice that the squaw is referred to as *he*: this is because there is no gender marking in most pidgins.

IV. Other pidgin features.
  A. *Sounds*.
   1. Pidgin sound systems are highly simplified. Even though there are only five vowel symbols in English, there are actually about eleven vowel sounds: *a* can stand for the *a* in *father* as well as the one in *cat*, for example. But a pidgin usually has only the "basic five" vowels, *a*, *e*, *i*, *o*, and *u*.
   2. Pidgins also drop the sounds in older languages that are harder to learn. Zulu of southern Africa, for example, is one of the Bantu languages that has some click sounds. There is a pidgin Zulu, called *Fanakalo*, that was developed by Africans from other regions brought in to work the mines in South Africa. Fanakalo speakers usually just replace the clicks with a *k*, as we would. Zulu has tones; Fanakalo does not.
  B. *Vocabulary*. Pidgins stretch their small vocabularies with circumlocutions. In Chinese Pidgin English, *goose* was *big fela kwak kwak maki go in wata*.
  C. *Reliance on context*. Pidgins do not have developed ways to distinguish among *When he came* versus *Although he came* versus *If he comes*, and so on. For example, there was a pidgin Eskimo. One sentence was *kim-mik ka'i-li pi-cu'k-tu*, which was, literally, "dog come want." This could mean any number of things depending on the situation in which it was said and the question it answered:

Eskimo Pidgin English:	
	kim-mik ka'i-li pi-cu'k-tu dog come want
Why are you whistling?	"Because I want the dog to come." "Because I want the dogs to come." "Because I want my dogs to come." "Because I want your dogs to come."
Why do you want Jim?	"Because I want him to bring me a dog."
Why are you locking the door?	"Because dogs keep trying to get into the house."
Why did Jim go to Fort MacPherson?	"Because he wants to get dogs there."

  D. In the Pacific Northwest, there was once a pidgin based on the Native American language Chinook called *Chinook Jargon*. Although the Indians in this region were known for being rather taciturn while speaking, when speaking Chinook Jargon, they were very animated in terms of expression and gesture, to compensate for the small resources in the pidgin.

V. Simple grammars in older languages versus pidgins.

  A. A question that may arise here is why a language such as Chinese, which also leaves much to context, is not a pidgin. The answer is that even languages without endings and that leave much to context remain complex in other ways.

  B. For example, recall that Chinese has tones, while pidgins do not. Chinese has the classifiers used with numbers, but Chinese Pidgin English used only one of these and then only sometimes. Chinese, like all languages, also has a large and subtle vocabulary. But no pidgin can distinguish such concepts as *nibble*, *bite*, *munch*, *gnash*, and *graze*.

VI. Pidgins, again, are not real languages. They are adults' partial versions of real languages. However, pidgins are important in providing the basis for new real languages, creoles. That is the subject of the next lecture.

Essential Reading:

Sebba, Mark. *Contact Languages: Pidgins and Creoles*. New York: St. Martin's Press, 1997.

Questions to Consider:

1. Have you ever spoken a foreign language at the pidgin level? Is there someone who you regularly speak to in, for example, Spanish, at a level just enough to "get by"? What parts of the language have you not mastered, and what kinds of concepts would you have trouble expressing?

2. American Indians really did often speak a pidgin English, although it was hopelessly implausible that Tonto never got beyond this level despite spending a lifetime by the Lone Ranger's side. However, in other cases, should the depiction of Indians speaking pidgin be avoided in order to discourage degraded conceptions of Native Americans' intelligence, or should the pidgin be shown out of a concern for historical accuracy?

Lecture Twenty-Eight
Language Starts Over—Creoles I

Scope: Only some new languages are truly new, having emerged when pidgin speakers came to use the pidgin as an everyday language. In these situations, people combine vocabulary from the language they are learning with grammar from this and their native languages, the result being a new hybrid rather than a dialect of the language that provides the words. These are creole languages and have emerged mostly amidst the slave trade and related activities. Jamaican patois, Haitian, and Cape Verdean are creoles, as is the Tok Pisin used in Papua New Guinea as a lingua franca among the hundreds of languages spoken there.

Outline

I. Introduction.
   A. As we have seen, there are no new languages in the strict sense. All of today's languages are continuations of earlier ones: English is one of today's versions of Proto-Indo-European.
   B. But there have been situations since the first language arose when people speaking pidgins, which are not real languages, have found themselves in situations where they needed to use the pidgin as their main language. In such situations, people build the pidgin into a new real language. This is called a *creole*, and creoles are the world's only truly new languages.

II. From pidgin to creole: The South Seas.
   A. In the late 1700s, when the English colonized Australia, they traded with Aboriginals there in a pidgin English. They continued using this pidgin as they extended their business to Oceania, using Melanesians in whaling and collecting sandalwood and sea cucumbers.
   B. This South Seas pidgin was typical of what we saw in the previous lecture: small vocabulary, elementary grammar. Here is an early sample:

South Seas Pidgin, 1835:

No! We all 'e same a' you! Suppose one got money, all got money. You—suppose one got money—lock him up in chest. No good! Kanaka all 'e same 'a one.

C. The English then established plantations in Queensland and elsewhere and brought men from Papua New Guinea and several islands in Oceania to work them on long-term contracts. Because the workers spoke several different languages, the South Seas Pidgin served as a lingua franca, now used daily for years. In addition, the men often continued using the pidgin when they went home, because so many languages are spoken in Papua New Guinea and on many Oceanic islands. Gradually, the pidgin was expanded into a real language.

D. One branch of this language is Tok Pisin, spoken today in Papua New Guinea alongside the hundreds of indigenous languages there.

   1. In South Seas Pidgin, tense was largely left to context, as in this sentence:

   South Seas Pidgin:

   You plenty lie. You 'fraid me se-teal. Me no se-teal, me come worship. What for you look me se-teal?

   2. But Tok Pisin, as a creole and therefore a full language, has the same kind of equipment for setting sentences in time as older languages, as we see here:

   Tok Pisin:

She goes to market.	*Em i go long maket.*
She goes to market (regularly).	*Em i **save** go long maket.*
She is going to market.	*Em i go long maket **i stap**.*
She has gone to market.	*Em i go long maket **pinis**.*
She went to market.	*Em i **bin** go long maket.*
She will go to market.	*Em **bai** go long maket.*

3. Tok Pisin also has a nuanced vocabulary. *Hevi* began meaning "heavy," but it has evolved semantically into also meaning "difficulty" and is used in idioms to mean sadness, as in *Bel bilong mi i hevi*, "I am sad."
   4. This, then, is a real language. Tok Pisin is used in the Papua New Guinea government and in newspapers. One can speak it badly or even decently but not well.

III. Creole: A generic term.
   A. Creoles are spoken throughout the world, wherever history has forced people to expand a pidgin into a full language. For example, in Louisiana, African slaves developed a creole based on French, just as South Seas natives developed one based on English. Louisiana blacks call this language *Creole*, but this is actually just one of dozens of creole languages. Creolization is a general process in language change.
   B. *Caribbean creoles*. For example, Louisiana Creole was but one of many creoles developed by African slaves brought to work plantations in the New World. Jamaican patois was one; Haitian Creole is another; Papiamentu of Curaçao is a creole based on Spanish. Most of the world's creoles were born in plantation or similar conditions.
   C. *Creoles elsewhere*. Creoles are also spoken on the West African coast, such as the ones created as the Portuguese explored and colonized there, starting in the 1400s. Cape Verdean is one of these. The Portuguese also left behind several creoles in India and Southeast Asia. Mauritian Creole is a French creole spoken on an island near Madagascar.
   D. *Folk terminology and "pidgin."* Some creoles are called "pidgin" by their speakers. Jamaican patois was transported to the West African coast in the 1800s and gave birth to several new creoles in Sierra Leone, Nigeria, and Cameroon. These are often called "pidgin," though they are actually real languages: creoles. An English creole was also born in Hawaii but is still called "pidgin" there.

IV. Creole versus dialect.

A. Because most of a creole's words are from the dominant language its creators learned, creoles can seem as if they are versions of that language (as their speakers often even suppose). But creoles actually use the words in grammars that are quite different.

B. For example, in English, one says *Where have you been?* In a nonstandard dialect of English, Black English, one says *Where you been at?*, but this is recognizable as a kind of English. However, in the creole English of Guyana, one says *Wisaid yu bin de?*, and in the creole English of Suriname called Sranan, one says *Pe i ben de?*

V. Where do creoles get their grammar?

A. Much of a creole grammar is based on the native languages of its creators. For example, in Sranan, *That hunter bought a house for his friend* is *A hondiman dati ben bai wan oso gi en mati*.

Sranan:

A	hondiman	dati	ben bai	wan	oso	gi	en	mati.
the	hunter-man	that	PAST buy	a	house	give	his	mate

"That hunter bought a house for his friend."

Sranan runs the verbs together in this way because the West African language many of its creators spoke, Fongbe, does the same thing:

Fongbe:

Koku	so	ason	o	na	e.
Koku	take	crab	the	give	her

"Koku gave her the crab."

B. Other parts of creole grammars appear exotic today but are actually just features of the regional dialects spoken by the whites with whom slaves had contact. For example, *Gullah* is a creole spoken on islands off of South Carolina. Gullah for *I come here every evening* is *Uh **blant** come yuh ebry eebnin*. This *blant* appears strange to us, but it comes from regional British dialects, such as the one of Cornwall we saw in Lecture Fourteen, which used *belong* in the same way: *Billee d' b'long gwine long weth 'e's sister*, "Billy goes with his sister."

C. In other ways, creoles revert to what many linguists think are innate grammar "defaults" that many or even most languages have drifted away from but lie at the base of our capacity for language. For example, no matter what the word order is in a creole creator's native language or the one that the creator is learning, a creole's word order is almost always subject-verb-object. Many linguists consider this order the basic one for language, even though all possible orders exist throughout the world.

Essential Reading:

McWhorter, John H. *The Power of Babel*. New York: HarperCollins, 2001 (chapter 4).

Sebba, Mark. *Contact Languages: Pidgins and Creoles*. New York: St. Martin's Press, 1997.

Supplementary Reading:

Roberts, Peter. *West Indians and Their Language*. Cambridge: Cambridge University Press, 1988.

Questions to Consider:

1. "Oh, creole—like in Louisiana. And the spicy food and voodoo…Spanish mixed in, right?" This is how laymen typically conceive of what *creole* means. Based on this lecture, how would you explain what a *creole language* actually is?

2. Creole-speaking nationalists often argue that the creole should be used in official contexts as a badge of local identity. More Eurocentrically oriented countrymen often object that the "high" language—English, French, or whatever—should be used officially because it is a conduit to the wider world and success within it. Where would you come down in such a debate?

Lecture Twenty-Nine
Language Starts Over—Creoles II

Scope: Creoles, as new languages, do not have the volume of frills that older ones do, but they have complexities that qualify them as "real languages." For example, Saramaccan Creole, spoken in Suriname by descendants of runaway slaves, has multiple words for "to be" depending on shade of being and a special way of marking that an act of throwing or pushing or falling ended instead of going on indefinitely. Like real languages, creoles change over time, have dialects, and mix with other languages. Creoles are based on the innate language ability of humans: children exposed to a pidgin will expand it into a creole spontaneously, as happened in Hawaii at the turn of the 1900s.

Outline

I. Creoles are real languages.

    A. Creoles can seem to be lesser versions of the languages they take their words from, a major reason being that a creole has few or none of the gender markers and conjugational endings that European languages have. But creoles actually have complexities of their own.

    B. *Saramaccan* was developed by African slaves who escaped plantations in Suriname and founded their own communities in the interior. Their descendants still live there today and speak a creole with words mostly from English, Portuguese, and Dutch and a grammar that splits the difference between English and Fongbe, spoken in West Africa.

    C. Here is a sentence in the language:

Nóɔ hɛ̃ wɛ wã dáka tééé dí mujɛ̃ɛ-mií fɛ̃ɛ̃, de bi tá kái ɛ̃ Jejéta.
then it-is one day long-ago the woman-child of-her they PAST "-ing" call her Jejeta

"Then one day long ago they were calling her daughter Jejeta."

    D. *Vocabulary*. There are words from five different languages in that one sentence. *De* is from *they*, *wã* is from *one*. But *dáka* is from

Dutch's *dag*. *Mujéɛ* is from Portuguese *mulher*. *Wɛ* is from Fongbe, and *tééé* is from Kikongo, a Bantu language.

E. *Sounds.*
  1. The sound marked as *e* is pronounced "ay" and the one marked ɛ as "eh"; similarly, *o* is pronounced "oh" while ɔ is pronounced "aw." Saramaccan does not have a basic pidgin-style sound system.
  2. The accent marks indicate tone, which Saramaccan has. Sometimes, tone is the only way to distinguish otherwise identical words, as in Chinese. *Kái* is *call*, but *kaí* is *fall*.

F. *Grammar.*
  1. Saramaccan has two verbs "to be" that work in a subtle way. *Da* is used to show that two things are the same thing: *Mi da Gádu*, "I am God." *Dé* is used to show where something is located—a different way of being, if you think about it—*Mi dé a wósu*, "I am at home." But then, this same *dé* is used to show that one thing is a type of something else: *Mi dé wã mbéti*, "I am an animal." This is as if being a kind of something were to be "in" it.
  2. I and my graduate students found that Saramaccan marks the end of a path an object follows after falling, being pushed, or jumping. The word *túwé* comes from *throw away*, but it is used in ways that seem redundant at first, such as in this sentence:

Mi	tótɔ	dí	águ	túwɛ	a	wáta.
I	push	the	dog	throw away	in the	water

"I pushed the dog into the water."

We get a clue as to what its function is with another sentence:

Vínde	dí	biífi	túwɛ.
throw	the	letter	throw

"Throw the letter in" (the trashcan).

The *túwɛ* is not being used in a literal sense but as a marker that something "made it" where it was aimed or headed. This is like the difference between *I threw it in the water* and *I threw it into the water*—the first sentence technically could mean that I was in the water while I threw it. But Saramaccan marks this distinction more clearly and regularly than English does.

G. *Change over time.* Like all languages, once creoles emerge, they start undergoing the same processes we have seen in this series.
  1. *Transformation.* In early Saramaccan, *kái*, "call," was *káli*. The *l* dropped out over time.
  2. *Dialects.* There are northern and southern dialects of Saramaccan. In the north, *not* is *á*. In the south, it is *ã*.
  3. *Mixture.* The slaves who created Saramaccan were exposed mostly to English and Portuguese, but the Dutch took over the country soon afterward in 1667, and Suriname was a Dutch colony for the next three centuries. Today, Saramaccan has a layer of Dutch words threaded throughout the language. The numbers 3, 5, 9, 11, and 12 are from Dutch, for example.

II. A new language in one generation.

A. Creoles show that humans are genetically programmed to use real language. Most creoles were gradually expanded from pidgins by adults over time. But in some situations, children exposed to a pidgin turn it into a creole.

B. American businesses established plantations in Hawaii in the late 1800s, staffing them with Portuguese foremen and workers from China, Japan, Korea, and the Philippines. The first generation of workers spoke a pidgin English with little grammar, as in:

Gud, dis wan. Kaukau enikain dis wan. Pilipin ailaen no gud. No mo mani.

"It's better here than in the Philippines—here you can get all kinds of food—but over there, there isn't any money [to buy food with]."

People often used word order according to their native language. Because Japanese puts verbs last, Japanese pidgin speakers often put the verb last in the pidgin. Languages of the Philippines put their verb first; thus, for example, a speaker of Ilocano would often put the verb first in the pidgin:

Japanese speaker:

Mi kape bai. "He bought my coffee."

Ilocano speaker:

Meri dis wan. "He got married."

C. But the children born to these workers in Hawaii streamlined and expanded the pidgin into a creole English (now still called "pidgin"), with the same rules used by all speakers whatever the language they were using at home. For example, the creole has full machinery for placing actions in time:

dei bai	they buy
dei bin bai	they bought
dei stay bai	they are buying
dei go bai	they will buy
dei bin stay bai	they were buying
dei go stei bai	they will be buying

D. This creole is now the casual language of Hawaii, spoken by people of various ancestries.

Essential Reading:

McWhorter, John H. *The Power of Babel*. New York: HarperCollins, 2001 (chapter 4).

Supplementary Reading:

Bickerton, Derek. *Language and Species*. Chicago: University of Chicago Press, 1990. (Includes a summary of the author's work on Hawaiian "pidgin" and its emergence [the source of the discussion here], as well as its implications for how language emerged.)

Simonson, Douglas (Peppo). *Pidgin to Da Max*. Honolulu: The Bess Press, 1981.

Questions to Consider:

1. Even creole speakers are often given to supposing that their languages are not "real" ones, partly because they are usually only rarely written and, in some ways, seem to be "baby talk" versions of the language most of their words come from. How might you explain to a creole speaker why his or her creole is, in fact, just as much "a language" as English?

2. Many argue that language is simply an outgrowth of humans' mental abilities and resist Chomsky's idea that we are specifically programmed to speak. Yet children do spontaneously expand a pidgin into a full language. Is this phenomenon compatible with resistance to the innateness hypothesis, or can we see the Hawaiian scenario as "Score one for Chomsky"?

Lecture Thirty
Language Starts Over—Signs of the New

Scope: Many linguists have argued that because creoles are real languages, they are not even identifiable as different from older languages unless we know their history. But in fact, creoles are the only languages that lack, or have very little of, the grammatical traits that emerge only over time. No creole marks shades of possession regularly, has gender markers distinguishing tables from chairs on the basis of sex, or has more than a little of the irregularities that bedevil us in learning older languages. In all of this, creole grammars are the closest to what the grammar of the first language was probably like.

Outline

I. Introduction.

   A. A question looming at this point is: if creoles are real languages, then how are they different from simple language mixture? The answer is that because creoles are new languages, they have not had time to amass the "mess" that we have seen in old languages.

   B. It has often been said that creoles are different from old languages only in terms of their history. But this is an oversimplification—creoles are more interesting than that.

II. How can we tell it's a creole?

   A. Most languages either have gender and conjugation markers, such as European languages, or tones, such as Chinese. As we have seen, these features develop over long periods of time by grammaticalization (gender, conjugation) or sound change (tones).

   B. Because they start as pidgins and grow from there, creoles are too young to have drifted into conjugation markers, Chinese-style tone, and so on. Thus, many creoles have none of these features, and none has more than a small amount.

   C. But this alone cannot tell us whether a language is a creole. We can point to a small number of old languages that, by chance, have neither gender or conjugation markers nor tone, in Polynesia, Southeast Asia, and West Africa.

D. But we can still tell a creole from these languages. In old languages, there are always prefixes and suffixes whose meaning is not always predictable. For example, *under-* in *underlie*, *undershoot*, and *underestimate* has the same meaning. But what does *under-* mean in *understand*? This kind of irregularity results from semantic change over long periods of time.

E. Because they are old, even languages without gender and conjugation markers or tone have their "understands." Chrau, of Vietnam, is one of these. Try to figure out what the prefix *pa-* means from the meanings of the words it is used in.

Chrau (Vietnam):

găn "go across"	*pagăn* "crosswise"
le "dodge"	*pale* "roll over"
lôm "lure"	*palôm* "mislead"
lăm "set, point"	*palăm* "roll"
jŏq "long"	*pajŏq* "how long?"

F. The only languages where there are very few or no "understands" are creoles. For example, *-pasin* (from "fashion," as in "way") has the same meaning with all of the roots it combines with:

Tok Pisin:

gut "good"	*gutpasin* "virtue"
isi "slow"	*isipasin* "slowness"
prout "proud"	*proutpasin* "pride"
pait "fight"	*paitpasin* "warfare"

III. Creoles: the world's sleekest languages.

    A. The absence of "understands," then, is one of many ways in which creoles are less needlessly complex than old languages. We have seen that creoles are by no means "ground zero" in terms of complexity, but they are closer to this than an old language can be.

    B. *Irregularity*. For example, creoles have very few or none of the irregular verbs that bedevil us in learning European languages. In English, we say *went* rather than *goed*, *was* rather than *be'd*, *sent* rather than *sended*. In Sranan, *went* is *ben go*, *was* is *ben de*, *sent* is *ben seni*, and so on.

IV. Hints of the first language.

A. Because creoles are the result of language starting anew, they shed light on what the world's first language was probably like.

B. Because gender and conjugation take time to appear, we can assume that the first language was one like creoles, or Chinese, in lacking these.

C. In the same way, because languages take time to wend into marking shades of possession, exactly how one learned of something, shades of subjecthood, and so on, we can assume that the first language did not have alienable possessive marking, evidential markers, ergativity, and similar traits.

D. Languages distinguish nouns, verbs, adjectives, and adverbs with prefixes and suffixes: *happy*, *happiness*, *happily*. Because affixes start as separate words and arise through grammaticalization over time, we can assume that in the first language, one word could often stand as a noun, verb, adjective, or adverb, as in languages today with few affixes, such as Chinese. Sranan creole is a language like this, where the word *hebi* can have many meanings:

Sranan Creole (Suriname):

A	saka	hebi!	A	hebi	e-hebi	mi!
the	bag	heavy	the	weight	is-weigh	me

"The bag is heavy! Its weight is weighing me down!"

E. Thus, while we most likely cannot know what the first language's words were, creoles give us the closest approximation of what its grammar would have been like.

Essential Reading:

McWhorter, John H. *The Power of Babel*. New York: HarperCollins, 2001 (chapter 5).

Questions to Consider:

1. Have you ever made up your own language? If you have—or if you were to—what aspects of grammar did/would you see as necessary after you worked out some basic words? You probably did not assign each word a gender, as in French or Spanish, but what kinds of features would you see as necessary?

2. If creoles are identifiable as a type of language at first, then over time, as they develop the weight of bells and whistles typical of older languages, they will not be identifiable as such. Is there a line to be drawn as to when a creole can be designated an "older" language? Or should creoles always be classed apart because of the type of social history they were born in?

Lecture Thirty-One
Language Starts Over—The Creole Continuum

Scope: "Creoleness" is a continuum concept. Some creoles are closer to the language that provided their words than others: Saramaccan is barely recognizable as a kind of English, but French creoles, such as the one of Mauritius, are more like French in their grammars. There are even semi-creoles that are poised between dialect and creole. Many creoles exist as continua of varieties, shading from the European language itself to one quite far from it, with no break in between. In bird's-eye view, this sheds light on what a "language" can be, such as Spanish, which shades across dialects into Portuguese while also existing in several creole varieties as well as the Spanish-Quechua hybrid Media Lengua, while Portuguese exists as several creoles plus semi-creole varieties in Brazil.

Outline

I. Just as one dialect shades into another one, leaving the concept of "language" an artificial and arbitrary one, "creoleness" is a continuum concept. Once we know this, we are in a position to put the finishing touches on our conception of how speech varieties are distributed across the globe.

II. Depth of creoleness.

    A. Some creoles are further from the language that provided their words than others. For example, although all of this Sranan sentence's words are from English, it is obviously quite a different language in all ways:

A	hondiman	dati	ben bai	wan	oso	gi	en	mati.
the	hunter-man	that	PAST buy	a	house	give	his	mate

"That hunter bought a house for his friend."

The sounds pattern in sequences of consonant-vowel-consonant-vowel, as in Japanese. Thus, *that* is *dati*, *mate* becomes *mati*. This is based on how sounds work in the African language Fongbe, as is the way the verbs are strung together and the placement of *dati* after *hondiman* instead of before.

B. But other creoles are closer to the language they are based on. In Mauritian Creole, *they were going* is the exotic-looking:

Mauritian Creole:

Zot	ti pe	ale
They	PAST "-ing"	go

"They were going."

Regional French:

eux-autres étaient après aller

But actually, this is largely a phonetic rendition of the sentence in the regional French the slaves were exposed to, *eux-autres étaient après aller*, "they were after going." Pronounced casually and rapidly, this sentence is quite like the Mauritian one. Mauritian is somewhat less creolized than Sranan.

III. Semi-creoles.

A. Some creoles are poised directly between a European language and true creoleness, neither exactly dialects of the European language nor languages like Tok Pisin. These have been called semi-creoles.

B. On the island of Réunion off the east African coast, in the 1700s, Malagasy people were brought as slaves to work small coffee plantations. They lived side by side with their white owners and spoke with whites as much as among themselves. In this kind of situation, what emerges is less a creole than a kind of abbreviated French—a more extreme version of what happened to English after the Viking invasions.

Réunionnais semi-creole French:

Alor	mon	papa	la	tuzur	di	amwen,
then	my	father	PAST	always	say	to-me
en	zur	kan	li	lete	zenzan…	
one	day	when	he	was	bachelor	

"Well, my father always said to me, one day when he was a bachelor…"

C. Réunionnais has no gender markers regularly, and no plural suffix and usually uses particles before the verb for tense, like typical creoles. But it is recognizable as "French" nevertheless in a way that Sranan and Tok Pisin are not recognizable as English.

IV. Creole continua.

A. Many creoles actually consist of a series of dialects, with one furthest from the European language and others shading ever closer, such that the "creole" is actually a series of shells expanding outward from a nucleus, as in the classic model of atoms.

B. For example, it can appear that there are so many ways to say *I gave him* in Guyanese creole that there appears to be no structure in the language. But actually, the versions can be aligned to show an increasing likeness to English:

Guyanese Creole: *I gave him*

mi bin gii am
mi bin gii ii
mi bin gi i
mi di gii ii
mi di gi hii
a di gii ii
a did gi ii
a did giv ii
a did giv hii
a giv ii
a giv im
a giv him
a geev ii
a geev him
I gave him

The most "creole" sentence has *mi* for *I* and uses the *bin* particle for past instead of the *-ed* suffix. As we get closer to Standard English, *did* is used instead of *bin*, which reflects a common way of expressing the past in regional British dialects of the past, and *a* for *I* differs from the standard only in pronunciation. Finally, we get to a sentence that is the standard one in a different accent.

- C. This kind of continuum is especially common in English creoles of the Caribbean, such as Jamaican patois, and is also true of Louisiana Creole and Cape Verdean. This often encourages speakers to view the creole as just a version of the European language (and, sadly, a "bad" one).

V. All the world is a continuum.
- A. As standard languages shade into dialects, dialects shade into creoles, while languages often shade into one another via chains of dialects. The sense a language map gives us of "languages" checkering the globe often corresponding to country boundaries, then, is highly misrepresentative (although inevitable).
- B. For example, "Spanish" is a bundle of dialects in Spain. Spanish shades into Portuguese through the Galician dialect(s). In the New World, there are hundreds of Latin American dialects of Spanish. In Ecuador, Spanish intertwined with Quechua and resulted in Media Lengua. There are two creole Spanishes in the New World, Papiamentu and Palenquero of Colombia, where Spanish began again mixed with African languages. In the Philippines, there is a dialect cluster of Spanish creoles. In the United States, a new dialect of Spanish is emerging that borrows heavily from English: Spanglish. Meanwhile, there are Portuguese dialects in Brazil, Africa, and Southeast Asia; the one in Brazil has semi-creole varieties as a legacy of its slave plantation beginnings. There are various Portuguese creoles in Africa, India, and Southeast Asia.
- C. The same kind of reality is true for a great many "languages" in the world. All people speak complex varieties of language, differing in clinal degree from one another and often not assignable as any one "thing."

Essential Reading:

McWhorter, John H. *The Power of Babel*. New York: HarperCollins, 2001 (chapter 4).

Sebba, Mark. *Contact Languages: Pidgins and Creoles*. New York: St. Martin's Press, 1997.

Supplementary Reading:

Roberts, Peter. *West Indians and Their Language*. Cambridge: Cambridge University Press, 1988.

Questions to Consider:

1. Because the progression from older language to creole is clinal, some argue that there should be no term *creole* at all; that is, in all cases, we are dealing with human language—period. How do you feel about drawing distinctions along what is actually a continuum? Is there any use in this, or is this an artificial distinction, along the lines of treating tomatoes as vegetables rather than the fruits that they actually are?

2. Many creolists' main mission has been to show that the apparent chaos of a continuum like the one in Guyana has structure—that creoles are indeed "language." If you were a specialist in creoles, would this be your main focus, or would you feel it urgent to share other information about creoles—and what?

Lecture Thirty-Two
What Is Black English?

Scope: This series allows us to gain a better understanding of Black English than was possible during, for example, the Ebonics controversy of 1996. Black English is a nonstandard dialect of English, with its own rules and complexities. It contains many features found in nonstandard English dialects of the United Kingdom, which slaves in America were exposed to in contact with settlers and indentured servants who spoke these varieties. Some have argued that Black English is an African language with English words, but this would make it a creole, and we can see that it does not have the traits of those languages. Rather, to the extent that it simplifies English a bit more than other dialects, Black English is lightly influenced by being created by adult learners—just as standard English itself was after the Viking invasions.

Outline

I. Before we proceed to the final four lectures, we are now in a position to understand the nonstandard English dialect most immediate—and controversial—for Americans. Because of the widely covered Oakland School Board controversy in 1996, it is now best known as Ebonics. Linguists have called it Black English or, more technically, African-American Vernacular English (AAVE).

II. Features.

  A. It is often thought that Black English refers only to slang, such as the colorful language well known from rap music. But this is only the surface. Black English is a distinct dialect of English on all levels.

  B. *Sounds.* For example, what is sometimes referred to as a "black sound" is due to a different sound system from the standard dialect's. This is often thought of as "leaving off sounds" because of how we spell English words but is often just a matter of using a different sound.

    1. For example, Black English has *wif* instead of *with*, but if you think about it, *th* is two letters but one sound. Norman French

has *carbon* while standard has *charbon*, but there is no *h* "left out" in Norman.
   2. In other cases, Black English's vowel is more complex than Standard English's. *Bill* in Black English is more like "beal."
C. *Grammar*. Black English has systematic grammatical differences from Standard English.
   1. *To be*. In places, Black English is simpler: *She my sister* is good Black English.
   2. *Habitual "be."* Elsewhere, Black English comes out ahead. To say *She be walkin' to the store* does not mean that she is doing it right now but that she does it on a regular basis. Standard English usually leaves this difference to context: to indicate regularity, Standard English uses the bare present—*She walks to the store*.

III. Is Black English an African language?
A. Some have argued that Black English is less English than an African, or African-derived, language with English words. However, these claims do not stand up to scrutiny.
B. Black English as African language.
   1. For example, especially in the context of the Oakland controversy, some proposed that Black English is based on African grammar, just as such creoles as Sranan and Haitian are. This claim is partly based on traits of Black English, such as the ability to use the same verb form with any pronoun: *he walk* instead of *he walks*. Many West African languages pattern like Chinese and have no endings.
   2. But Black English does not match up with any African grammar the way creoles do. For example, no African-American would say *The hunter that been buy one house give his friend*.
   3. Black English also retains too much of English's "mess" to qualify as a creole, such as irregular verbs (*stood, went*) and plurals (*men, feet*).
C. Black English as a creole continuum.
   1. Others have argued that Black English began as a creole, namely Gullah, and that a continuum formed between Gullah and Standard English. Black English would now be in the

middle of that continuum, while Gullah itself remains only in the Sea Islands and somewhat inland.

2. But there are many problems with this idea. There is no historical evidence of Gullah spoken anywhere far beyond where it is today. There were blacks who migrated to other countries in the 1800s when they supposedly would have been speaking Gullah, but the descendants of these blacks do not speak anything like Gullah even when English itself is not spoken in the country (such as the Dominican Republic).

IV. Black English as British dialect?

A. In fact, many of the features we associate with black American speech are found in regional Englishes in the United Kingdom.

B. Habitual *be* is used by Irish English speakers, and black slaves learned it from indentured servants who spoke this dialect. *Even when I be round there with friends, I be scared* is good Hiberno-English.

C. Black English uses *it* where the standard uses *there* in such sentences as *It's somebody at the door*. We see parallels to this in good old Cornwall: *'Tes some wan t'the dooar*.

V. What is Black English, then?

A. Yet the fact remains that there is an obvious difference between Black English and the English of the rural Brit. For example, there is no British dialect where *She my sister* is typical. There are also other features where Black English simplifies the standard, such as in not switching the order of subject and auxiliary in questions: *Why you didn't call me?* instead of *Why didn't you call me?*

B. Although Black English hardly "undoes" English enough to qualify as a creole or even semi-creole, there are enough traits like the above to show that the people who created Black English streamlined it slightly. We would expect this of African slaves learning the language quickly outside of a school setting. We would also expect in this situation that Africans would have left a slight impact from their accent—the hardest thing to shed when speaking a second language—on their rendition of English. Hence, certain aspects of the black "sound," as distinct from the British accent.

C. Thus, Black English can be described as a semi-semi-semi-creole of regional English dialects of the United Kingdom, standing in a relationship to Standard English rather like English does to Old English.

Essential Reading:

McWhorter, John H. *Word on the Street: Debunking the Myth of a "Pure" Standard English*. New York: Perseus, 1998 (chapters 6–7). (A more detailed, but accessible, exposition of the topics in this lecture.)

Supplementary Reading:

Rickford, John Russell, and Russell John Rickford. *Spoken Soul: The Story of Black English*. New York: Wiley and Sons, 2000.

Questions to Consider:

1. In 1996, the Oakland School Board proposed that black American students be taught in Black English as a bridge to acquiring Standard English, arguing that Black English is an African language with English words, different enough from the standard to pose a barrier to black children's learning to read. After this lecture and the course so far, what are your views on this? Even if you suppose that the school board harbored some exaggerated notions, do you think that there was some truth in their perspective? Why or why not?

2. The temptation is great to hear young blacks' speech as "bad grammar." Yet this lecture and many previous ones suggest a certain challenge: listen to the rawest speech of this kind that you can find—rap lyrics or youngsters chatting in public. Can you wrap your head around the fact that they are not using "bad grammar" in any logical sense? Cockney English is one thing, but to Americans, this is largely rather "cute"—try to really bring it home!

Lecture Thirty-Three
Language Death—The Problem

Scope: Just as extinction is part of the natural history of life forms, it is also common in the life cycles of languages. Throughout human history, languages have died because of invasions and migrations, and more so as agriculture made these phenomena more common. But today, there is an extinction crisis among languages, just as among life forms: a language dies every two weeks, and 90 percent of the current 6,000 will likely be extinct by 2100. Once a generation stops passing a language to its children, a language is on its way to no longer being spoken. As it dies, a language begins reverting to pidgin form, losing its endings, the richness of its vocabulary, and the nuances that distinguish a full language.

Outline

I. This series has been about a process of growth, mixture, rebirth, and extravagance. But another part of the natural history of language is decline and extinction, just as with flora and fauna.

II. How languages die.

   A. When one generation of speakers does not speak the indigenous language(s) to the next one on a regular basis, then the new generation acquires only an incomplete version of the language, often almost a pidginized form.

   B. This generation cannot pass the language on to the next one at all and, thus, the language is no longer spoken. This means that even in a situation where great numbers of old people speak a language, if most middle-aged people do not, then the language is severely endangered.

   C. Unlike animals and plants, which leave fossils, when a language dies without being recorded, it is truly dead, with no hope of recovery. And even when we have records of the language (epics, inventory lists, sayings, songs), this is but an approximation of what the language in its totality was.

III. A natural process—to an extent.

   A. Languages have died throughout time, when their speakers are exterminated or, more frequently, subordinated by a more powerful group and switch to the new group's language. We have seen Hittite and Tocharian as dead Indo-European languages. There are dozens of such languages known in the Eurasian region alone.

   B. The process accelerated with the development of agriculture and the Neolithic revolution. Before this, humans existed in hunter-gatherer groups, possibly speaking tens of thousands of languages. But agriculture creates food surpluses that increase population and encourage migrations and subjugation of other groups. As a result, migrators' languages tend to extinguish the ones they encounter.

   C. But the process is occurring today at a vastly accelerated rate. Ninety-six percent of the world's people speak one of the 20 most spoken languages (Chinese, English, Spanish, Hindi, Arabic, Bengali, Russian, Portuguese, Japanese, German, French, Punjabi, Javanese, Bihari, Italian, Korean, Telugu, Tamil, Marathi, and Vietnamese). According to one estimate, 90 percent of the world's 6,000 languages will be extinct by 2100.

   D. For example, there were about 300 languages spoken in the continental United States four centuries ago. Today, a third of them are spoken by no one, and of the remaining two-thirds, only a handful are being passed on to new generations, while all the rest are spoken only by very old people and will be dead within a decade.

IV. What happens to a language when it is dying?

   A. When a language stops being used regularly, it starts to be spoken in a way that shaves off much of the fascinating machinery that defines human language. That is, it starts to revert to a pidgin-like stage, making do with less.

   B. *Vocabulary.* By the 1980s, the Cayuga language of New York State had a word for *leg*, *foot*, and *eye* but not for *thigh*, *ankle*, or *cheek*. The original word for *enter* was no longer used, with *go* as a substitute. This is reminiscent of the small vocabulary in such pidgins as Russenorsk.

C. *Affixes*. In Spanish, it is easier for an English speaker to say *voy a hablar*, "I'm going to talk," instead of *hablaré*, using the future ending. In the same way, in dying languages, speakers start avoiding prefixes and suffixes of this kind, preferring to use separate words that are easier to remember. In Pipil of Central America, there was a future ending -*s*, but today's speakers prefer to use their *go* verb.

D. *Articulateness*. In many Native American languages, rendering what we think of as sentences as single words is common, and deciding when to do it is part of truly speaking the language with nuance. In Cayuga, to say *She has a big house* one says "It big-houses her," *Konǫhsowá:neh*. But the speakers of the dying version today tend to just say the Cayuga version of *Her house is big*. That is, they speak Cayuga with the soul of English.

E. The generation after the one that speaks the language on this level usually knows a few words or phrases in the language but cannot carry on a conversation at all. At this point, the language is no longer spoken.

Essential Reading:

Crystal, David. *Language Death*. Cambridge: Cambridge University Press, 2000.

Supplementary Reading:

Nettle, Daniel, and Suzanne Romaine. *Vanishing Voices: The Extinction of the World's Languages*. New York: Oxford, 2000.

Questions to Consider:

1. Are you an immigrant to this country whose children speak your native language—but not quite in the same way that you do? Likely they sprinkle English words into their version of the language more than you did when you were young. But what about their grammar? Does their version of the language show any of the signs of language death above?

2. Some people think it would be a good thing if the world spoke only one language (to aid communication); others hope to save all 6,000 (for the sake of diversity). Many would fall somewhere in between. Where would you fall, and what kinds of languages would you prefer to see saved?

Lecture Thirty-Four
Language Death—Prognosis

Scope: There are many movements to revive dying languages, such as Welsh, Irish Gaelic, and Maori, but success is elusive. As speakers of indigenous languages come together in cities, it is unlikely that they will pass these on to their children. People often see their unwritten native language as less "legitimate" than written ones used on television, in radio, and in films. In addition, indigenous languages tend to be complex and quite unlike the usually European ones that dominate the world. Most likely, in the future, many languages will die, while others will live as "taught" languages, encountered in school and on the page rather than learned at home.

Outline

I. Language revival movements.

   A. There is increasing awareness that there is an extinction crisis among the world's languages, just as there is among living creatures. There are thriving efforts to pass along to new generations Irish Gaelic, Welsh, and Breton (all Celtic languages), as well as Maori and Hawaiian (the Polynesian language originally spoken in the islands).

   B. Some people involved in these efforts are more optimistic than others. As to the question of whether we can maintain 6,000 languages as spoken ones, the truth, as it so often does, lies in the middle. There is little prospect that English will become the world's only language (remember how common diglossia and bilingualism are worldwide). But there is equally little possibility of maintaining all the world's languages for longer than another century.

II. Obstacles to keeping 6,000 languages alive: It has been said that once there is a revival movement, the language is already dead. This may be too pessimistic, but it is grounded in sad truths.

   A. *Status*. Often, people who speak a "top 20" language alongside an indigenous one do not think of their native language as "real,"

because it is not written or used in wider communications. Thus, linguists and anthropologists are often more interested in preserving a community's language than its members are.

B. *Urbanization.* The general trend for indigenous people to relocate to cities (or be forced there) helps exterminate indigenous languages. If parents speaking different languages have children in the city, the parents are unlikely to pass both, or even one, of the languages on to their children, and even if they try, the city's lingua franca will likely be their children's main language. And whatever they learn of their parents' language, these children certainly will not pass this on to their own children.

C. *Tainted goods.* By the time a language is dying, often most of the people speaking it are no longer using the full vocabulary or grammar. Unless the language has been exceptionally well documented already, much of what the actual language consisted of may already be lost to history.

D. *Difficulty.*
1. Another obstacle to reviving languages is that languages under threat are usually spoken by small numbers of people and were rarely learned by outsiders. As we have learned in this series, these languages tend to be extremely complex. Rare is the threatened language whose grammar requires only the effort that Spanish or Dutch would to master.
2. Threatened languages also tend to be from groups other than the Romance and Germanic ones that we are most familiar with, such that in the threatened language, the very basics of putting words to thoughts are vastly different from ours. The problem is that speakers of the dying language have become most comfortable in Romance and Germanic languages. In Mohawk, for example, *Suddenly, she heard someone give a yell from across the street* is *Tha'kié:ro'k iá:ken' ísi' na'oháhati iakothón:te' ónhka'k khe tontahohén:rehte'.* Literally, this is "Suddenly, by what you could hear, there, it's beyond the street, the ear went to who just then made-shouted back towards her."

III. The success story: Hebrew. Revivalists often look to the successful revivification of Hebrew from a liturgical written language to a spoken one as a sign that such movements have promise. But Israel was a unique circumstance: it was a new land entirely; its immigrants spoke several languages and needed a lingua franca; the language had been richly preserved in writing; and the use of Hebrew was associated with a powerful religious impulse. These things are not true of any other situation where there are revival movements.

IV. Predictions.

    A. *Taught language versus spoken language.* As times goes on, many languages will survive more as second languages than as first ones. It is more common than educated Westerners generally know for people to speak a language or two decently if not perfectly, having learned a new language for trade or work after childhood. My sense from the Irish, Welsh, Breton, Maori, and Hawaiian movements is that the languages are unlikely to be passed on to children again in enough households to be significant, but that the languages nevertheless can live as "taught" languages, rather as many Americans have a decent if not native-level proficiency in Spanish.

    B. *Documented languages.* A great many languages, however, will only survive on paper. The chances of reviving most of the Native American or Australian Aboriginal languages would seem nonexistent, which makes it imperative that they at least be described and recorded for posterity.

V. In this series, you have seen that linguistics is not about blackboard grammar or translation or learning to speak a lot of languages. If the topics I have taken you through have been interesting and your life circumstances allow it, you might consider helping to preserve a dying language in some way. You could contact the linguistics department nearest to you for advice.

Essential Reading:

McWhorter, John H. *The Power of Babel*. New York: HarperCollins, 2001 (chapter 7).

Supplementary Reading:

Abley, Mark. *Spoken Here: Travels among Threatened Languages*. Boston: Houghton Mifflin, 2003.

Questions to Consider:

1. One linguist has argued his reluctance to disagree with a father who speaks a dying language in supporting his son in moving to the big city to seek his fortune, even though this will mean that the son will not pass the language on to his children. Languages are marvelous, but then exotification is perhaps a luxury of the fortunate. Then again, idealism is fundamental to change. Discuss.

2. I once had the experience of teaching some Native Americans who no longer spoke the language of their ancestors the basics of that language. It was hard—the language's sounds were unnatural to an English speaker, the word order placed the verb at the end, and the grammar as a whole was strikingly different from English's. Learning a language such as Spanish is hard enough, but it was clear to me—and to them—that in the end, the best we could do was give them a few words, such as numbers and family members, and some set expressions, including *Hello*. In your opinion, was this worth the effort, and why or why not?

Lecture Thirty-Five
Artificial Languages

Scope: There have been many attempts to create languages for use by the whole world. Some have been too needlessly complex, such as the briefly successful Volapük; others have been rather delightfully silly, such as Solresol, based on musical pitches. But Esperanto, a kind of streamlined Romance language, has had some success since its creation in 1887. Sign languages for the deaf are also artificial languages, but genuine ones, with grammar, nuance, and dialects, even created anew by deaf children if they are exposed to random collections of creative gesticulations.

Outline

I. Creoles are new languages that were created largely unconsciously, but many languages have been created deliberately. These languages, whether they succeed or pass away after a brief existence, are one more part of the natural history of language.

II. Artificial spoken languages.
   A. *Volapük*.
      1. The first influential artificial language was called Volapük, invented in 1879 by a Bavarian priest. It was based on Romance and Germanic, with 40 percent of the vocabulary English.
      2. It had a brief vogue, but it was based on a mistaken sense that the difficulties of old languages were necessary rather than accidents. Volapük was difficult to learn, with a complex series of endings and umlauted vowels. *Vola* was "world" and *pük* was "speak."

      Volapük:

      The Lord's Prayer

      O Fat obas, kel binol in süls, paisaludomöz nem ola...

      "Oh our Father, who art in heaven, hallowed be thy name…"

B. *Esperanto.*
1. In 1887, Ludovic Zamenhof, who had been struck by the animosity between cultures speaking Russian, Yiddish, German, and Polish as he was growing up in Bialystok, invented Esperanto, with a mostly Romance and Germanic vocabulary.
2. Esperanto has had some success. There are at least a million speakers, a literature, and translations, including the Bible, the Koran, and *Hamlet*.
3. Part of this success is the result of Esperanto's user-friendly structure. It is strictly regular and has only 16 formal rules.
4. Nouns end in *o*, adjectives in *a*, adverbs in *e*, and verb infinitives in *i*. Thus, *varma* is "warm," *varmo* is "warmth," and *varmi* is "to warm up." Present tense is indicated with the ending -*as*, past with -*is*, future with -*os*, conditional with –*us*, and imperative with -*u*. Suffixes create new words: *koko* is "rooster" and *kokino* is "hen"; *arbo* is "tree" and *arbaro* is "forest."
5. Esperanto does have a bias toward European languages, such as assuming that a language must have a marker for direct objects or the conditional. Here is a sample, which you might probably be able to make sense of even without familiarity with the language:

Esperanto:

Simpla, fleksebla, praktika solvo de la problemo de universala interkompreno, Esperanto meritas vian seriozan konsideron.

"A simple, flexible, practical solution to the problem of universal understanding, Esperanto deserves your serious consideration."

C. *Solresol.*
1. No discussion of artificial languages would be complete without a quick look at Solresol, invented in France in the early 1800s. It was based on musical pitches, which could be sung or whistled or played, as well as spoken. Related sequences of pitches were assigned to related words.
2. DORE was "I"; DOMI was "you"; DOREDO was "time"; DOREMI, "day"; DOREFA, "week"; DORESOL, "month";

DORELA, "year"; DORESI, "century"; MISOL was "good"; SOLMI was "bad."

III. Sign language.

    A. The signing of deaf people is not simply a series of gestures. Sign languages are actual languages, with a grammar of their own, that must be carefully learned. There are dozens of sign languages. America's is called American Sign Language, or ASL, but Britain has a different one, as do other countries.

    B. Most of the signs do not mean what an outsider might suppose, just as the correspondence between a barking mammal and the sequence of sounds d-o-g is arbitrary. For example, to convey the sign for "home" you must hold the tips of the fingers and thumb of one hand together, place them against one side of the mouth, and move them back toward the ear. That is obviously not the sign we would spontaneously come up with for the word, nor would we spontaneously know, upon seeing the sign, what it in fact means. ASL has about 4,000 signs.

    C. The world's sign languages parallel spoken ones in their "natural history." Many of today's sign languages trace, at least partly, to one created in France in 1775 at a school for the deaf. This, then, was a kind of Proto-World for sign language. Sign languages have dialects, as well.

    D. In being new languages, sign languages can be seen as creoles. Just as children exposed to a pidgin will expand it into a full language, in Nicaragua in the 1980s, deaf children at a school where each child was using gestures in an individual way created a systematic new sign language in one generation.

    E. Like creoles, sign languages have simpler grammatical structure than most older languages. This is due not only to the youth of the languages but also to the fact that facial expression can perform some of the work that spoken languages need words for. Nevertheless, sign languages have their more complex aspects, such as having classifiers according to shape that Chinese and other languages have.

    F. As creoles develop dialect continua toward a dominant language, some varieties of ASL are more affected by English than others. There are also various systems for writing ASL, although it remains primarily a spoken language.

Essential Reading:

Crystal, David. *The Cambridge Encyclopedia of Language*. Cambridge: Cambridge University Press, 1987. ("Artificial Languages"; section six, "The Medium of Language: Signing and Seeing").

Flodin, Mickey. *Signing Illustrated: The Complete Learning Guide*. New York: Perigee, 1994.

Supplementary Reading:

Richardson, David. *Esperanto: Learning and Using the International Language*. El Cerrito, CA: Esperanto League for North America, Inc., 1988.

Questions to Consider:

1. Part of the reason that Esperanto appears unlikely to become the world's universal language is that we effectively already have one: English. Is this a suitable state of affairs, or would we be better off with a more neutral universal language rather than an imperial—and complex—one?

2. Some people in the deaf community have argued against giving deaf children cochlear implants, arguing that this will discourage them from joining the deaf culture, including fluent signing. In our moment, this position is based partly on flaws in cochlear implant technology. But assuming that the technology improves, what is your opinion on the complex issue of encouraging the use of sign language—now the vehicle of theatrical pieces and poetry—as the badge of a cultural identity?

Lecture Thirty-Six
Finale—Master Class

Scope: By themselves, word histories are a kind of butterfly collection. But now, we can examine an English sentence etymologically and perceive how the word histories represent the processes of language change and mixture worldwide. In *While the snow fell, she arrived to ask about their fee*, there is a riot of hidden history: grammaticalizations, vast layers of borrowings, single meaningless sounds that used to be whole words we will never know, rules that began as accidental byproducts of other ones now extinct, words that began as multi-word idioms in other languages, and even fascinating mysteries.

Outline

I. Introduction.

   A. Many of you may have expected that the subject of this series would occasion more reference to words' histories. I have resisted dwelling on these too much, out of a sense that only after we have a full conception of how inherent change is to language can these etymologies be understood as more than isolated "just so" stories.

   B. But now that we are at the end of our journey, it will be useful to take a simple sentence of English and examine the extent to which it is but one snapshot along an endless process of mutation. The histories of the words are now useful to us in illuminating how this has happened in various ways.

   C. Our sentence is:

   While the snow fell, she arrived to ask about their fee.

II. Word by word.

   A. *While* is an example of grammaticalization. In Proto-Indo-European, it was a verb $k^w ei\partial$-, "to rest." In Old English, this verb became a noun, *hwīl*, meaning a peaceful stretch of time (we still say *spend a while* in this meaning). But after this, it became a grammatical word, showing that one thing happened within the same span of time as another. This grammatical meaning came from the part of *hwīl* referring to time, rather than rest. Today's *while*, then, has completely lost the connotation of rest that *kʷeiə-* had.

B. *The* is another grammaticalization, coming from the Old English word for *that*. To say *the cat* is to point out a certain cat, as opposed to *a cat*, which refers to any cat. But to say *that cat* is to be even more forcefully specific. The meaning of *that* weakened to *the* over time. This means, however, that Old English—and Proto-Indo-European—were languages like Chinese and legions of others that have no articles. *The* is a frill that English has drifted into, seeming as peculiar and superfluous to many foreigners as alienable possessive marking is to us.

C. *Snow* is an ordinary English word that has had its meaning for eons. However, the first *s* is a mystery. Other Indo-European languages have it in their *snow* word, too, but Latin's word *nix* lacked the *s*; thus, we have *neige* in French and *nieve* in Spanish. We might think that the *s* just dropped off in Latin. But in other cases, Latin has an *s* where one of its sisters doesn't. Latin has such words as *specit* for "sees," but in Sanskrit, this is *páçyati*. Indo-Europeanists call this *s* that floats in and out of the family *s-mobile* and think it was the remnant of a prefix. We will never know what the prefix was or its meaning, but we utter its remains whenever we say that it's snowing.

D. *Fell* is evidence of a suffix that is completely gone.
  1. If we made up a language on the spot, we would be unlikely to decide that the way to mark the past would be to change a verb's vowel. This happens in a language only by accident over time, because the vowel in some past suffix on the end of the word changes how people pronounce the vowel within the word. For example, before English had emerged, the plural of *foot* used to be *fōti*. But speakers would anticipate pronouncing the "ee" sound by pronouncing the "oh" sound close in the mouth to where "ee" is pronounced. This made the word "FAY-tee." Because final vowels are so fragile, the *-i* dropped off and left just "fayt." Then, the Great Vowel Shift changed this to *feet*. We assume that there was originally some sound like this after *fell*, but now, it is lost to the ages.

    2. But then recall from Lecture Twenty-Five that such verbs as *fall* may also change their vowels to mark the past because of ancient mixture with a Semitic language. It could be that when we say that the temperature fell, this is a legacy from people whose descendants now live in Tel Aviv, Cairo, and Addis Ababa.

E. *She* is a strange case as well. The Old English word was *hēo*, which was not pronounced the way it was spelled ("hey-oh") but as "hey-uh." But it is not a usual process in sound change for *h* to become a *sh* sound. One possible explanation refers to the fact that Old English still had three genders, so that there were three forms of the definite article, masculine *sē*, feminine *sēo*, and neuter *þæt*. Maybe people began associating *hēo* with this feminine *the*: after all, in Old English, to see several girls and say of one of them, *That one is wearing green*, one would say *sēo* is wearing green. Maybe there was a short step from this to changing *hēo* to *sēo*. One reason speakers may have made this change is that the word for *he*, pronounced "hay" then, was becoming hard to distinguish from "hay-uh."

F. *Arrive* is a borrowed word from French; we would be surprised if every word in this sentence traced back to Old English.
    1. The native word is *come*, and as often, the French word is more formal than the original English one, as with *pig* versus *pork*.
    2. *Arrive* actually started as an idiomatic expression in Vulgar Latin. *Ad rīpam* meant "to the shore" in Latin, and *adrīpāre* was, therefore, a created verb, as if we were to say "I got-to-the-shored." *Adrīpāre* became *arrīpāre* as the *d* became more like the *r* it came before (remember assimilation from Lecture Three?), and in Old French, the word was *ariver*. We borrowed it from French and have no idea that we are mouthing a Vulgar Latin neologism when we say *arrive*!
    3. And as for the past ending -*ed*, some linguists think that it began as the word for *did* in early Germanic ("I arrive-did"). This means that *arrived* contains the remnants of three words from two different languages.

G. *To* goes back to Old English *tō*, and the reason we pronounce it with an "oo" is the same reason that a word pronounced "fode" is now pronounced *food*: the Great Vowel Shift.

H. *Ask* traces back to an Old English word *āscian*, but despite how we feel about the pronunciation "aks" today, in Old English *ācsian* was as common as *āscian*, casually written in formal documents. As so often, our contemporary senses of what is "wrong" are arbitrary—even literate English speakers once saw nothing amiss in the alternation between these words.

I. *About* came from a case of the rebracketing that we saw create the word *alone* in Lecture Four (the *arrive* case is another one). *At* plus *by* plus *out*, pronounced together rapidly over time, became the single word *about*, just as *God be with you* became *Goodbye*.

J. *Their* is not an original English word but one of the many words that the Vikings gave us. Why we switched to *their* (!) word instead of our own *hiera* is unknown.

K. *Fee* has a nice story. It, too, is not originally English—quite.
   1. We took it from Norman French's word *fie*, which started as *fief*, and French had, in turn, borrowed this word from the language of Germanic-speaking invaders (the Normans were, in fact, originally *Norsemen*, Vikings who had stayed on the continent). Thus, English borrowed a word through French from one of its own sister languages.
   2. The Proto-Germanic word had been **fehu*. But this, in turn, was an example of the strange consonant changes of Grimm's Law that, for example, changed Indo-European *p*'s, such as the *p* Latin has in *pater*, into the *f* of *father*. The Proto-Indo-European word was **peku*, and it meant *wealth* or *property*. That root came through more intact in Latin, in words we later borrowed, such as *pecuniary*. Thus, *fee* and *pecuniary* (and *peculiar*) trace to the same root!

III. We see that any sentence of English is, viewed up close, a petri dish of disparate elements stewing together, testaments to a long history of one of the first language's 6,000 living branches and its endless mutations and mixings with other branches. Of course, we can see similar stories in any sentence from any of the 6,000 languages in the world. I hope to have demonstrated what a wonder the world's languages are when viewed as dynamic and symbiotic systems in a constant flux that is here predictable, but there surprising. Under this perspective, language, rather than being a basket of words knit together by a collection of "rules" that we learn in school and usually fall short of, is one of the many wonders of being members of our species.

Questions to Consider:

1. How will you feel the next time you get that e-mail that has been making the rounds for years asking why English is so illogical? One of the aims of this course has been to elucidate the degree to which any modern language is the product of a great deal of contingent and endless mutation of an original template. Have I succeeded?

2. Overall, how has your perspective on language changed after the lectures in this course? Are you equipped to provide insights on language issues of the day at parties? Have you been reinforced in views you held before or coaxed into new ones?

Language Maps

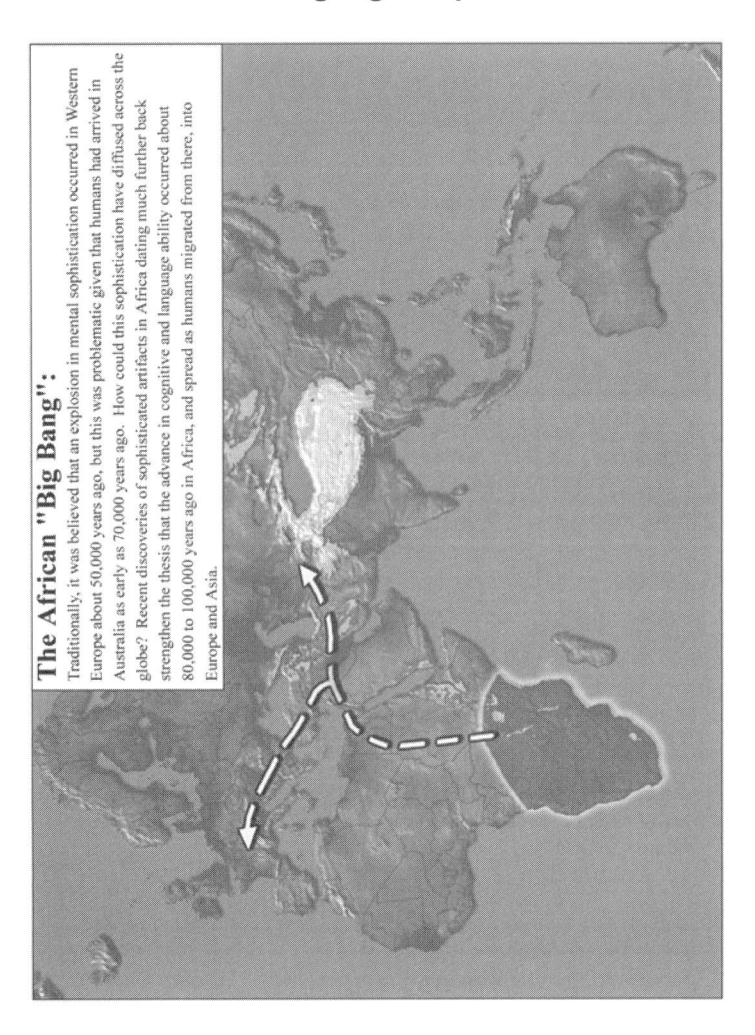

The African "Big Bang":

Traditionally, it was believed that an explosion in mental sophistication occurred in Western Europe about 50,000 years ago, but this was problematic given that humans had arrived in Australia as early as 70,000 years ago. How could this sophistication have diffused across the globe? Recent discoveries of sophisticated artifacts in Africa dating much further back strengthen the thesis that the advance in cognitive and language ability occurred about 80,000 to 100,000 years ago in Africa, and spread as humans migrated from there, into Europe and Asia.

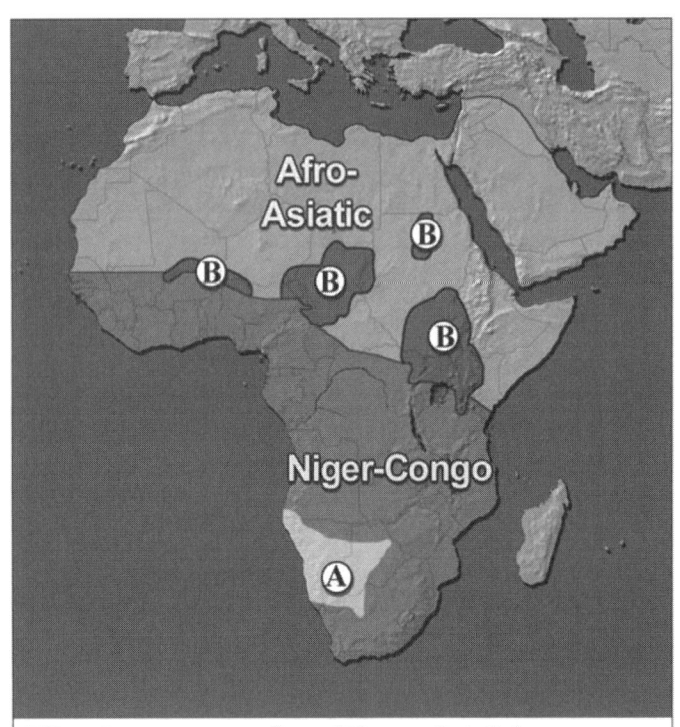

The language families of Africa

Niger-Congo: The language family most predominant in sub-saharan Africa, it includes the Bantu subfamily, which includes such languages as Zulu and Swahili.

Afro-Asiatic: The language family most common in the northern half of Africa, and extending into Arabia and the Middle East, it includes the North African Berber subfamily and the Cushitic (e.g., Somali), Chadic (e.g., Hausa), and Semitic subfamilies. Semitic languages include Arabic and Hebrew.

Khoi-San or "click" languages (A): These are concentrated in Namibia, and parts of South Africa and Botswana, and may be related to the first spoken languages.

Nilo-Saharan (B): Spoken in parts of Chad, Sudan, Ethiopia, Mali, Uganda, and Kenya.

The Indo-European Family

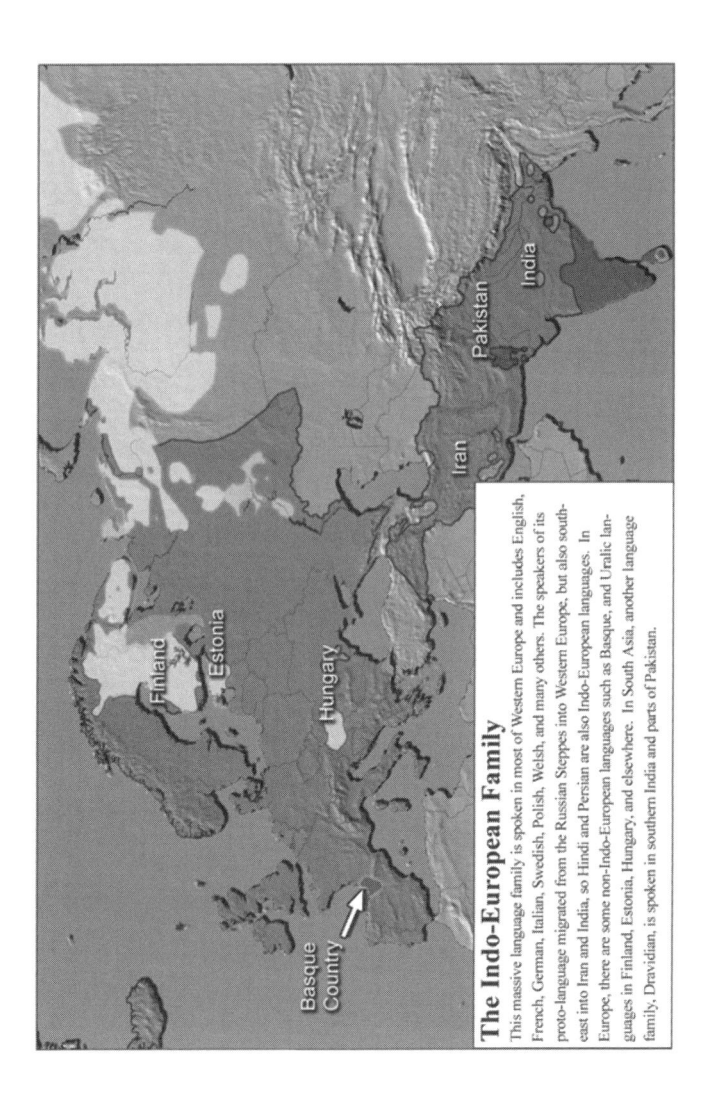

This massive language family is spoken in most of Western Europe and includes English, French, German, Italian, Swedish, Polish, Welsh, and many others. The speakers of its proto-language migrated from the Russian Steppes into Western Europe, but also southeast into Iran and India, so Hindi and Persian are also Indo-European languages. In Europe, there are some non-Indo-European languages such as Basque, and Uralic languages in Finland, Estonia, Hungary, and elsewhere. In South Asia, another language family, Dravidian, is spoken in southern India and parts of Pakistan.

The "Sinosphere":

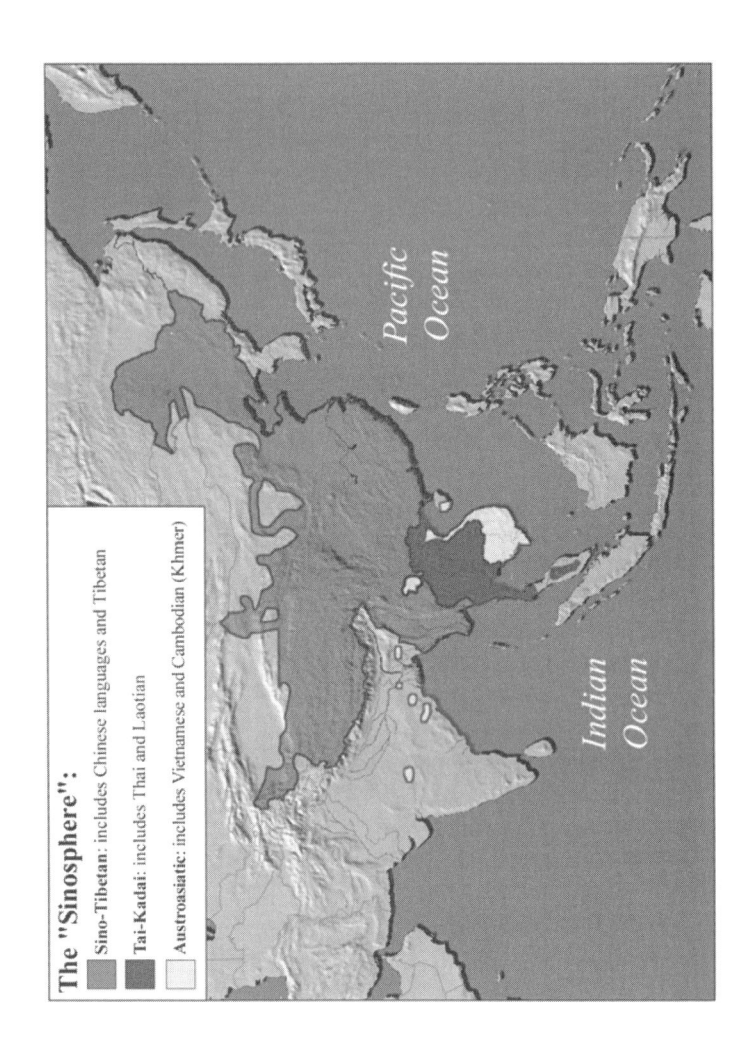

Sino-Tibetan: includes Chinese languages and Tibetan

Tai-Kadai: includes Thai and Laotian

Austroasiatic: includes Vietnamese and Cambodian (Khmer)

Pacific Ocean

Indian Ocean

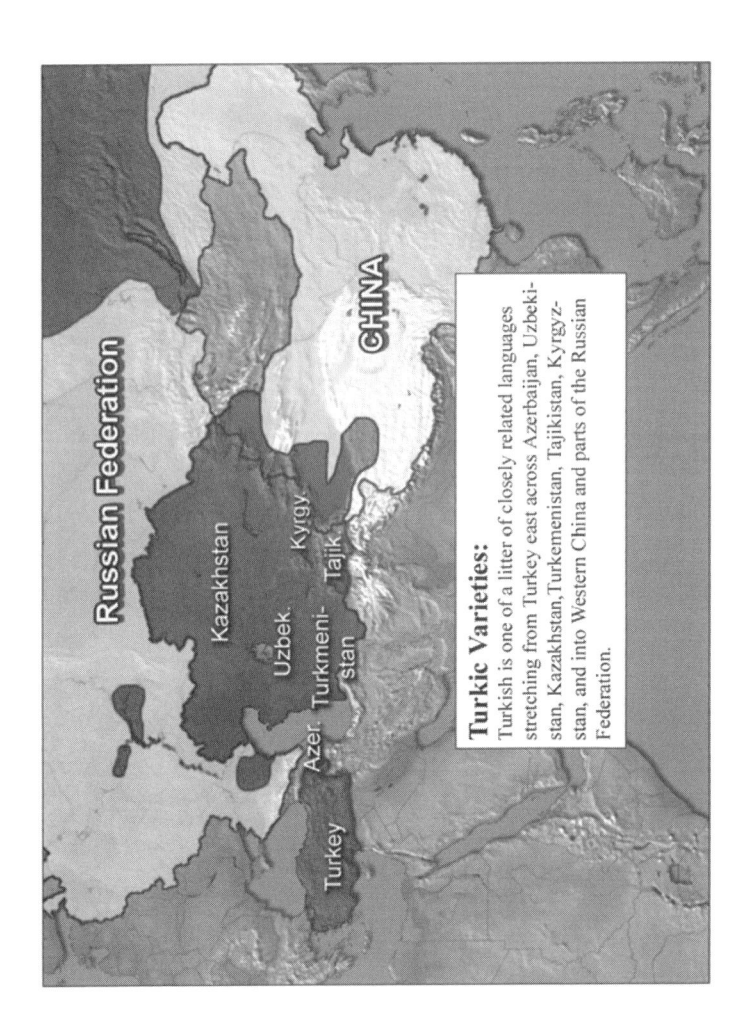

Turkic Varieties:
Turkish is one of a litter of closely related languages stretching from Turkey east across Azerbaijan, Uzbekistan, Kazakhstan, Turkemenistan, Tajikistan, Kyrgyzstan, and into Western China and parts of the Russian Federation.

Timeline

150,000–80,000 B.C.	Estimated time during which human language arose.
4000 B.C.	Probable origin of Proto-Indo-European.
3500 B.C.	First attested writing.
3000 B.C.	Probable origin of Semitic.
2000 B.C.	Bantu speakers begin migrations south and eastward.

A.D.

450–480	First attestation of English.
787	First Scandinavian invasions of England.
mid-1300s	Beginning of the standardization of English.
1400	Beginning of the Great Vowel Shift in English.
1564	Birth of William Shakespeare.
c. 1680	The origin of Saramaccan creole.
1786	Sir William Jones gives first account of Proto-Indo-European.
1887	Ludwig Zamenhof creates Esperanto.
c. 1900	The birth of Hawaiian Creole English.
1916	Discovery of Hittite.

Glossary

Algonquian: Family of Native American languages spoken in Canada and the northern and northeastern United States, including Cree, Ojibwa, Shawnee, Blackfoot, Fox, and Kickapoo. Much work has been done on the reconstruction of Proto-Algonquian.

alienable possessive marking: Distinguishing things possessed as objects (alienably) from those possessed as parts of one's body or as personal intimates (inalienably), e.g., *my chair* versus *my mother*. Many languages have different possessive pronouns for these two situations or distinguish between them in various other ways.

Amerind: One of the three families into which Joseph Greenberg divided the notoriously variegated hundreds of Native American languages. Amerind is by far the biggest of the families, comprising most of the languages native to the Western Hemisphere.

Areal: Of or pertaining to an area or region.

assimilation: The tendency for a sound to become similar to one adjacent to it: Early Latin *inpossibilis* became *impossibilis* because *m* is more like *p* than *n*, in requiring the lips to come together.

Austroasiatic: The Southeast Asian language family that includes Vietnamese and Khmer (Cambodian).

Austronesian: The massive Southeast Asian and Oceanic language family that includes Tagalog (Filipino), Indonesian, Javanese, Malagasy, and Polynesian languages, such as Hawaiian and Samoan.

Baltic: The small subfamily of Indo-European today including only Lithuanian and Latvian, the closest languages in the family to the Proto-Indo-European ancestor.

Bantu: The 500 languages spoken in sub-Saharan Africa, of which Swahili and Zulu are the best known; a subfamily of the Niger-Congo family.

Broca's area: The area of the brain, above the Sylvian sulcus on the left side, that is thought to control the processing of grammar.

Celtic: The subfamily of Indo-European including Irish Gaelic, Welsh, and Breton, all now under threat; the family once extended across Europe.

Chinook Jargon: The pidgin based on Chinook and Nootka with heavy admixture from French and English, used between whites and Native Americans in the Pacific Northwest, most extensively in the 19th century.

classifiers: Equivalents to *head* in such English expressions as *three head of cattle*, used more regularly in many languages, usually after numerals, and varying according to shape or type of noun (long, flat, round, and so on). Many languages, such as Chinese ones, have dozens of such classifiers.

code-switching: When speakers regularly alternate between two languages while speaking, including in the middle of sentences.

comparative reconstruction: The development of hypothetical words in a lost proto-language of a family of modern languages through comparing the words in all the languages and deducing what single word all could have developed from. This is also done to reconstruct prefixes, suffixes, and sentence structure.

creole: The result of the expansion of a reduced version of a language, such as a pidgin, into a full language, which usually combines words from a dominant language with a grammar mixing this language and the ones the creole's creators spoke natively.

creole continuum: The unbroken range of varieties of a creole extending from one sharply different from the language that provided its words ("deep" creole) to varieties that differ from the dominant language largely in only accent.

critical-age hypothesis: The observation that the ability to acquire language flawlessly decreases sharply after one's early teens, first explicated by Eric Lenneberg in 1967 but since then referred to extensively by the Chomskyan school as evidence that the ability to learn language is innately specified.

diglossia: The sociological division of labor in many societies between two languages, or two varieties of a language, with a "high" one used in formal contexts and a "low" one used in casual ones. The classic cases are High German and Swiss German, practically a different language, in Switzerland, and Modern Standard Arabic, based on the language of the Koran, and the colloquial Arabics of each Arabic-speaking region, such as Moroccan and Egyptian, which are essentially different languages from Modern Standard and as different from one another as the Romance languages.

double negative: The connotation of the negative in a sentence via two negator words: *I ain't seen nothing*.

Dravidian: A family of languages spoken mostly in southern India, including Tamil and Kannada, separate from the Indo-Aryan languages spoken elsewhere in the country.

equilibrium (vs. punctuation): A state when many languages share space in constant contact with one another, with no language threatening any other one to any significant extent over a long period of time. Linguist R. M. W. Dixon proposes this as human language's original state, contrasting with *punctuation* in which speakers of one language migrate and conquer other peoples, spreading their language across large areas.

ergativity: The condition in which a language marks subjects with different prefixes, suffixes, or separate particle words depending on whether the subject acts upon something (*He kicked the ball*) or just "is" (*He slept*). In ergative languages, if the subject does not act upon something it takes the same marker as the object, while subjects that act upon something take a different marker. Ergativity is rather as if in English we said *Him saw* instead of *He saw* in a sentence without an object, but then said *He saw her* when there was an object.

Esperanto: A language created in the late 19th century by Ludwig Zamenhof, who hoped it would help foster world peace; comprised largely of words and grammar based on Romance languages, but made maximally simple. Esperanto has been the most successful of many artificial languages.

Eurasiatic: A "superfamily" proposed by Joseph Greenberg comprising Indo-European, Uralic (e.g., Finnish and Hungarian), Altaic (e.g., Turkish, Mongolian), Dravidian, Kartvelian (of the Caucasus mountains), Afro-Asiatic (e.g., Arabic, Hausa), Korean, Japanese, Chukchi-Kamchatkan (of eastern Russia), and Eskimo-Aleut. The Eurasiatic hypothesis differs from the Nostratic hypothesis in that the latter is based on comparisons of the families' proto-languages while the former is based on more general cross-family comparisons.

evidential markers: Markers that indicate how one learned a fact being stated (i.e., seen, heard, suspected, and so on); all languages have ways of expressing such things, but in some languages, one *must* express them with each sentence.

FOXP2 gene: The gene that is connected to humans' ability to speak, also found in slightly different form in chimpanzees and found to be damaged in a family in which a speech defect (specific language impairment) was common.

gender marking: The distribution of nouns into two or more classes, masculine and feminine usually included; the term usually refers to this as applied to inanimate objects, as well as animate ones, such as German's *der Löffel*, *die Gabel*, and *das Messer* for the spoon, the fork, and the knife.

Germanic: A subfamily of Indo-European including German, Dutch, Yiddish, Swedish, Icelandic, and English, distinguished by how very close Icelandic is to Proto-Germanic and how strikingly far English is from it.

grammatical words (vs. concrete words): Words that have no concrete essence but perform grammatical functions in a sentence, such as *would* or *then* or, well, *or*. These are as crucial as concrete words in making human language what it is.

grammaticalization: The development of a word from a concrete one into a grammatical one over time, such as French's *pas* from meaning "step" to "not." Grammaticalization is how most grammatical words, as well as prefixes and suffixes, come into being.

Great Vowel Shift: The transformation of many English vowels into other ones in the 1400s, before which many English spelling conventions had already gelled. This is why *made* is spelled as if it were pronounced "MAH-deh," which at a period before the Great Vowel Shift, it was.

Grimm's law: A curious transformation in the consonants of Proto-Germanic, in which Proto-Indo-European *p* became *f* (hence, Latin *pater*, English *father*), *t* became *th* (Latinate *tenuous*, original English *thin*), and so on.

Indo-Aryan: The subfamily of Indo-European including Hindi, Bengali, Gujarati, and other languages descended from Sanskrit.

Indo-European: The language family now occupying most of Europe, Iran, and India, likely originating in the south of present-day Russia; its proto-language has been reconstructed, called Proto-Indo-European.

Indo-Pacific: The family of languages including the several hundred spoken on New Guinea and some others spoken on nearby islands; the group is often termed Papuan. Relationships among the languages have only begun to be worked out.

inherent reflexive marking: The extension of reflexive marking (*I hurt myself*) to verbs indicating emotion, movement, and other processes done to or occurring within one's self: German *ich erinnere mich*, "I remember myself," for "I remember"; similarly, French *je me souviens*. Especially common in Europe.

intertwined language: Languages developed by people with a bicultural identity that neatly combine the grammatical structure of one language with words from another one, in various fashions; e.g., Media Lengua and Mednyj Aleut.

Italic: The subfamily of Indo-European that included Latin and is now represented by the Romance languages; Latin's relatives, such as Oscan and Umbrian, are long extinct.

Khoi-San: The family of languages spoken in regions of southern Africa best known for their click sounds; perhaps the world's most ancient language family.

laryngeals: The breathy sounds reconstructed by Ferdinand de Saussure as having existed in Proto-Indo-European, to explain why many of its reconstructed roots were "open-ended" ones with a long vowel and no final consonant. De Saussure was proven correct when such sounds occurred in the places he predicted in Hittite, an extinct Indo-European language discovered in documents in the early 20th century.

Media Lengua: An intertwined language spoken in Ecuador, with Quechua endings and word order and Spanish words.

Mednyj Aleut ("middle" Aleut): An intertwined language, now basically extinct, spoken by children of Russian traders and Aleut women on one of the Aleutian islands starting in the 19th century.

Miao-Yao: A family of languages spoken by isolated groups in South Asia, including Hmong. Presumably, the family was much more widespread before Chinese peoples migrated southward.

Moldovan: A variety of Romanian spoken in Moldova, a country adjacent to Romania formerly incorporated into the Soviet Union. Only this history leads Moldovan to be considered a separate language from Romanian in any sense.

Normans: The French people who took over England in the 11th century, speaking the Norman dialect of French, which profoundly influenced the English vocabulary. Norman was derived from Norsemen, that is, Vikings.

Nostratic: A "superfamily" proposed by Russian linguists Aron Dolgopolsky and Vladislav Illich-Svitych comprising Indo-European, Uralic (e.g., Finnish, Hungarian), Altaic (e.g., Turkish, Mongolian), Dravidian, Kartvelian (of the Caucasus mountains), and Afro-Asiatic (e.g., Arabic, Hausa). See also Eurasiatic.

particle: A short word that is not an ending or a prefix that has a grammatical function.

perfect construction: A construction separate from the ordinary past one, connoting that a past event still has repercussions in the present. *I have decided not to take the job* implies that the impact of the decision is still ripe; *I decided not to take the job* sounds more like recounting a long-past occurrence. This is especially common in Europe.

pidgin: A makeshift, reduced version of a language used by people with little need or inclination to master the language itself, usually for purposes of trade. If used as an everyday language, a pidgin can become a real language, a creole.

poverty of the stimulus: The Chomskyan argument that actual speech is full of mistakes and hesitations and rarely offers demonstrations of various rules of a language that children nevertheless master early; Chomsky and others argue that this supports the idea of language as an innate faculty.

prescriptivism (vs. descriptivism): The school of thought that prescribes how language ought to be (e.g., *Billy and I went to the store* is "better" than *Billy and me went to the store* because *I* is a subject), as opposed to the descriptivist approach, which simply describes how language is naturally (the latter fundamental to academic linguistics).

Provençal: The Romance variety of southern France closely related to French. Formerly the vehicle of the music of the troubadours, now represented by modern relatives, such as Occitan, threatened by French.

rebracketing: The redrawing of boundaries between words or parts of words as a result of plausible mishearings, such as *nickname* developing when speakers heard the original word *ekename* used after an indefinite article: *an ekename* became *a nickname*.

Riau Indonesian: A colloquial dialect of Indonesia spoken on the island of Sumatra with unusually little overt grammatical apparatus, leaving more to context than most known languages.

Russenorsk: A pidgin spoken especially in the 1800s between Russians and Norwegians trading during summers, neatly splitting the difference between Russian and Norwegian.

Sapir-Whorf hypothesis: An idea developed especially by Benjamin Lee Whorf speculating that differences between languages' grammars and vocabularies may channel how their speakers think, creating distinct views of the world.

Saramaccan: A creole language spoken in the Suriname rain forest by descendants of slaves who escaped into the interior and founded their own communities; the creole mixes words from English, Portuguese, Dutch, and the African languages Fongbe and Kikongo and has a grammar highly similar to Fongbe's.

Schwäbisch: A dialect of German spoken in the south of Germany, one of the many that is different enough from High German as to essentially be a different language.

semantic broadening: The development over time of a word's meaning into one more general: *bird* once referred to small birds but now refers to all birds.

semantic drift: The tendency for words' meanings to morph gradually over time to the point that the distance between the original meaning and the current one can be quite striking: *silly* used to mean *blessed*.

semantic narrowing: The development over time of a word's meaning into one more specific: *hound* once referred to all dogs but now refers to only a subset of them.

semi-creole: Languages not quite as different from a standard one as a creole is but more different than the typical dialect of that standard language. The French of Réunion Island, further from French than, for example, Canadian French but hardly as different from it as Haitian Creole, is a typical semi-creole.

Semitic: A language family spoken in the Middle East and Ethiopia including Arabic, Hebrew, and Amharic; most famous for its three-consonant word skeletons (K-T-B means "write" in Arabic; thus, *kataba*, "he wrote"; *maktab*, "office"; and so on).

Sinosphere: Linguist James Matisoff's term for the language area in Eastern and Southeastern Asia, where several separate language families have come to share several structural traits, such as tone, over the millennia because of constant contact.

Sino-Tibetan: A language family including Chinese, Tibetan, Burmese, and many other languages spoken in Southern and Southeast Asia; tone is common in the family.

sound shift: The tendency for sounds to change their articulation gradually and become new ones; the Great Vowel Shift in English is one example, as is the increasingly common pronunciation of *aw* as *ah* in America (*rah fish* instead of *raw fish*).

specific language impairment: The condition discovered in an English family in the 1980s, in which sufferers spoke rather slowly and hesitantly and often made errors usually made by foreigners. Those afflicted were found to have a faulty FOXP2 gene.

Sprachbund: An area where separate languages have come to share many grammatical features as the result of heavy bi- and multilingualism over time. A classic case is found in the Balkans, where Albanian, Romanian, Serbo-Croatian, Macedonian, Bulgarian, and Greek have become a Sprachbund. Of late, the term *language area* is becoming increasingly prevalent.

standard dialect: The dialect out of language's many that happens to become the one used in writing and formal situations, typically developing a larger vocabulary and norms for written, as opposed to spoken, expression.

SVO: The word order subject-verb-object, such as in English; SOV order is actually more common worldwide.

Tai-Kadai: A language family of Southeast Asia including Thai, Laotian, and lesser known languages, such as Shan.

Tocharian: An extinct Indo-European language once spoken by white peoples who migrated eastward to China, known from Buddhist manuscripts discovered in Central Asia.

Tok Pisin: An English pidgin spoken in Papua New Guinea, now spoken as a native language by many and, thus, a creole; one of the few such languages used commonly in writing and in the government.

Tsez: A language spoken in the Caucasus Mountains in Asia, typical of languages in this area in having an extremely complex system of sounds and grammar.

Volapük: An artificial language created by Johann Schleyer in the 19th century based on a European pattern; initially popular but less user-friendly than Esperanto, which quickly replaced it as the most popular artificial language.

Wernicke's area: The area of the brain, below the Sylvian sulcus, that is thought to control the processing of meaning.

Bibliography

Abley, Mark. *Spoken Here: Travels among Threatened Languages*. Boston: Houghton Mifflin, 2003. Abley subscribes too much to the Sapir-Whorf perspective for my taste, but this book provides vivid descriptions of assorted language revival movements, giving nicely balanced assessments of their likelihoods of success.

Arlotto, Anthony. *Introduction to Historical Linguistics.* Boston: University Press of America, 1972. An especially clear introduction to comparative reconstruction of proto-languages, often assigned in undergraduate courses some years ago. Newer books in the vein have come along, but this one is worth seeking in a library for its conciseness because the newer ones cover the historical linguistics field more broadly.

Bailey, Richard. *Nineteenth-Century English*. Ann Arbor: University of Michigan Press, 1996. A useful examination of how English just a little more than a century ago was more different from today's than one might suppose. The chapter on slang also gives a useful portrait of the "underbelly" of English so difficult to glean from most writings before the 1960s.

Baker, Mark. *The Atoms of Language*. New York: Basic Books, 2001. This complements Steven Pinker's *The Language Instinct* in describing an area of inquiry pursued by syntacticians working in the Chomskyan school in accessible terms. Pinker's classic is, ultimately, somewhat challenging in its length, while this one hews to a more compact point.

Barber, Elizabeth Wayland. *The Mummies of Ürümchi.* New York: W.W. Norton & Co., 1999. An accessible account of the discovery of historical evidence of the Tocharian-speaking people, knitting the linguistic issues into archaeology and history.

Baugh, A. C., and T. Cable. *A History of the English Language*. Englewood Cliffs, NJ: Prentice-Hall, 1978. One of those deathless staple sources, a standard, accessible history of English for those hungry for the details but not the trivia.

Bickerton, Derek. 1995. *Language and Human Behavior.* Seattle: University of Washington Press, 1995. A collection of lectures filling out the author's theory about human "proto-language" and its implications for how language began.

———. 1990. *Language and Species*. Chicago: University of Chicago Press, 1990. Argues that human language began with a "proto-language" substrate now preserved in the language ability of apes, infant speech, and pidgins, incorporating the author's pioneering theories about the birth of an English creole in Hawaii (there termed "Pidgin").

Bodmer, Frederick. *The Loom of Language*. New York: W.W. Norton, 1944 (paperback edition, 1985). Getting a little long in the tooth—not much on Third World languages—but remains a valuable compendium of data on many of the world's "grand old" languages, with a comparative focus. Still in print after 60 years for a reason.

Bryson, Bill. *The Mother Tongue: English and How It Got That Way*. New York: William Morrow and Co., 1990. Unsurpassed as a jolly, often laugh-out-loud trip through the history of English. Baugh and Cable will give the details, but this is a great introduction.

Burgess, Anthony. *A Mouthful of Air: Language, Languages…Especially English*. New York: William Morrow and Co., 1992. Burgess intended his tour of the world's languages as a primer for teaching us how to master them. I fear he was a bit idealistic on that goal, but he was a marvelous tour guide nonetheless and was less obsessed with Europe than writers in his vein back in the day.

Calvin, William H., and Derek Bickerton. *Lingua ex Machina: Reconciling Darwin with the Human Brain*. Cambridge, MA: MIT Press, 2000. A leading neurophysiologist and a specialist in language origins join forces in an engaging discursive exchange about how language began, within the framework of modern syntactic theory. Both are born teachers—a nice ride.

Cavalli-Sforza, Luigi Luca, and Francesco Cavalli-Sforza. *The Great Human Diasporas*. Cambridge, MA: Perseus Books, 1995. A general-public summary of what Luigi Cavalli-Sforza has discovered about human migrations in antiquity, using relationships between language families as support.

Chafe, Wallace, and Jane Danielewicz. "Properties of Spoken and Written Language," in *Comprehending Oral and Written Language*, edited by Rosalind Horowitz and S. Jay Samuels, pp. 83–112. New York: Academic Press, 1987. This article illuminates in clear language the differences—often shocking—between how we actually talk and how language is artificially spruced up in even casual writing, showing that spoken language, despite its raggedness, has structure of its own.

Comrie, Bernard, Stephen Matthews, and Maria Polinsky, eds. *The Atlas of Languages*. New York: Facts on File, 1996. One of several tours of the world's languages now available, especially useful for its maps, charts, and diagrams; attractively laid out. A nice introduction to the Indo-European languages, including the folk tale in full.

Crystal, David. *The Cambridge Encyclopedia of Language*. Cambridge: Cambridge University Press, 1987. An invaluable encyclopedia, lavishly illustrated, on anything one might want to know about language and languages. This selection has been at arm's length from my desk for 10 years now.

———. *The Cambridge Encyclopedia of the English Language*. Cambridge: Cambridge University Press, 1995. A magnificent, almost imposingly rich trip through English past and present in all of its facets, as beautifully illustrated as the volume described directly above. Captures between two covers a magnificent volume of information, much of it otherwise hard to access.

———. *Language Death*. Cambridge: Cambridge University Press, 2000. The crispest and most down-to-business of the various treatments of this topic released recently, by an author personally familiar with the travails of the Welsh revival movement.

Dalby, Andrew. *Dictionary of Languages*. New York: Columbia University Press, 1998. A feast of information on any language one might want to know about, clearly written and utilizing countless obscure sources. Especially good on writing systems and history.

Deacon, Terrence W. *The Symbolic Species: The Co-Evolution of Language and the Brain*. New York: W.W. Norton & Co., 1997. The most detailed account of the neurological perspective on the origins of language, representing a common view among such specialists that language "rides" on more general cognitive abilities. Many generative syntacticians would disagree, but Deacon's is an especially comprehensive argument from the other side.

Diamond, Jared. *Guns, Germs, and Steel*. New York: W.W. Norton & Co., 1997. Diamond's now classic account of why some societies have acquired more power than others incorporates ample information about how languages have spread across the globe, admirably accurate as well as readable.

Dixon, R. M. W. *The Rise and Fall of Languages*. Cambridge: Cambridge University Press, 1997. A muscular little monograph arguing that languages typically stew amongst one another in one place, becoming increasingly similar, and that only post-Neolithic migrations have led some languages to travel and give birth to brand-new offshoots taking root in new lands. The dedicated layman will glean much from the argument, which parallels Stephen Jay Gould's on punctuated equilibrium.

Dyer, Donald L. *The Romanian Dialect of Moldova*. Lewiston, NY: Mellen Press, 1999. A readable account of a "language" that is really just a minor dialectal variant of Romanian and how the confusion arose.

Ferguson, Charles A. *Language Structure and Language Use* (essays selected and introduced by Anwar S. Dil). Palo Alto, CA: Stanford University Press, 1971. Ferguson wrote his seminal work when linguists still wrote important work in a style accessible to interested readers; this essay of 1959 remains the classic introduction to the subject.

Finegan, Edward. *Language: Its Structure and Use*. Fort Worth, TX: Harcourt Brace, 1989. A textbook that combines layman-friendliness with detailed surveys of certain issues, such as the Polynesian languages and their history. I have used this one for years to usher undergraduates into the linguistic frame of mind.

Flodin, Mickey. *Signing Illustrated: The Complete Learning Guide*. New York: Perigee, 1994. This is an especially esteemed introduction to sign language for those stimulated by the subject.

Geertz, Clifford. "Linguistic Etiquette," in *Sociolinguistics*, edited by John Pride and Janet Holmes, pp. 167–179. Harmondsworth, England: Penguin, 1972. A classic and readable article on layers of language in Java—and, by analogy, the fashion in which a language varies according to social factors, divested of the loaded sociological implications that, inevitably, coverage of this subject referring to dialects closer to home tends to entail.

Goody, Jack, and Ian Watt. "The Consequences of Literacy," in *Literacy in Traditional Societies*, edited by Jack Goody, pp. 27–84. Cambridge: Cambridge University Press, 1968. This is a truly magic piece that shows how the sheer fact of language written on the page transforms consciousness and history. It's long but thoroughly readable and worth the commitment.

Grillo, Ralph. *Dominant Languages: Language and Hierarchy in Britain and France*. Cambridge: Cambridge University Press, 1989. A solid coverage of how standard English and standard French became what they are, rather than the marginal dialects that they were at their inception. For those interested in a closer look at a process usually described in passing, this is a good place to look, although available only in university libraries.

Halliday, M. A. K. "Spoken and Written Modes of Meaning," in *Comprehending Oral and Written Language*, edited by Rosalind Horowitz and S. Jay Samuels, pp. 55–82. New York: Academic Press, 1987. A useful comparison of the spoken and the written, which like the Chafe and Danieliwicz article, highlights a difference that is easy to miss.

Hockett, Charles F. "The Origin of Speech." *Scientific American* 203 (September 1960). This article is still useful in getting down to cases as to what distinguishes human speech from the fascinating but "not quite it" renditions of language seen in parrots, apes, and even dogs. Few have done it better since.

Hopper, Paul J., and Elizabeth Closs Traugott, eds. *Grammaticalization*. Cambridge: Cambridge University Press, 1993. Grammaticalization has been commonly discussed among linguists for only about 20 years, and this is the leading textbook on the subject. It is rather compact and written in terms that will not overly tax the interested layman.

Kaye, Alan. "Arabic," in *The World's Major Languages*, edited by Bernard Comrie, pp. 664–685. Oxford: Oxford University Press, 1990. Kaye writes in a distinctly "human" way in a book intended as drier than what he submitted. This is a nicely readable introduction to Arabic and its structure.

"Languages of the World." *Encyclopedia Brittanica*. 1998 edition. This chapter, nowadays festooned with gorgeous, crystal-clear color maps, has been one of my own staples since I was 13. It covers the language families of the world in admirable and authoritative detail.

Lucy, John A. *Language Diversity and Thought: A Reformulation of the Linguistic Relativity Hypothesis*. Cambridge: Cambridge University Press, 1992. For those with a serious interest in the "Does language channel thought?" hypothesis that so often intrigues laymen, this monograph summarizes and critiques all of the relevant sources and experiments on the Sapir-Whorf hypothesis up to its publication. (There have been a few studies slightly more promising for the hypothesis since.)

Matisoff, James. "On Megalocomparison." *Language* 66 (1990): 106–120. A cool-headed objection to Proto-World and related theories by a linguist who pulls off the feat of writing academically respectable linguistics papers in prose reasonably accessible to the layman, including a puckish sense of humor.

Matthews, Stephen. *Cantonese: A Comprehensive Grammar*. London: Routledge, 1994. Reference grammars can be forbidding to those outside academia, but this one is relatively accessible, as well as admirably detailed.

McWhorter, John. *The Power of Babel*. New York: HarperCollins, 2001. The basic thesis of this course, that human language is a natural history story, just as the evolution of animals and plants is, is encapsulated in this book. Solely as a result of lack of competition, the book is unique in giving a tour of human language from a modern perspective, including recent developments in the study of language change and how languages color one another.

———. *Word on the Street: Debunking the Myth of a "Pure" Standard English.* New York: Plenum Publishing, 1998. In this book, I attempt an argument that there is no such thing as "bad grammar," using Black English as a springboard but also addressing bugbears of the "Billy and me went to the store" type. There is also a chapter on how Shakespearean language is less accessible to us than we often suppose, useful in illuminating the subtleties of how languages change.

Nettle, Daniel, and Suzanne Romaine. *Vanishing Voices: The Extinction of the World's Languages*. New York: Oxford, 2000. As informed as David Crystal's *Language Death* but also founded on a sober (if, in my view, sadly unlikely) political argument for those interested in this view on the subject.

Norman, Jerry. *Chinese*. Cambridge: Cambridge University Press, 1988. A compact survey of Chinese in its "dialectal" variety, easy to read, trimming most of the fat (although one might skip the details periodically), and in print.

Ong, Walter. *Orality and Literacy: The Technologizing of the Word*. London: Routledge, 1982. A readable and invaluable classic exploration of the impact on the human experience created by something as seemingly mundane as the encoding of speech in written form; truly eye-opening and one of my favorite books.

Oppenheimer, Stephen. *The Real Eve: Modern Man's Journey out of Africa*. New York: Carroll & Graf, 2003. A survey of recent genetic evidence tracing human migrations, including evidence of higher-level mental activity further back in time than traditionally supposed by those pursuing a "Big Bang" 30,000 years ago. This is an updated report on the topic of Cavalli-Sforza's classic book: a bravura detective story, only occasionally tiring the non-specialist a bit.

Pei, Mario. *The Story of Language*. Philadelphia: J.B. Lippincott, 1949. Now available only on the library shelf but worth a read; this grand old "The World's Languages" trip inspired many a linguist (including myself). Put on your historical-perspective glasses and savor an old-fashioned scholar's best of his many books for the public.

Pepperberg, Irene Maxine. *The Alex Studies: Cognitive and Communicative Abilities of Grey Parrots*. Cambridge, MA: Harvard University Press, 2002. Battling the skeptics, Pepperberg tells us about her uncannily articulate parrots. Push aside the arcane and the dry and marvel at how human a pop-eyed bird can seem.

Pinker, Steven. *The Language Instinct*. New York: HarperPerennial, 1994. This is the classic introduction to what many linguists do in the modern world, examining whether there is an innately specified ability to use language in our brains. Pinker writes with hipness and wit.

Ramat, Anna Giacalone, and Paolo Ramat, eds. *The Indo-European Languages*. London: Routledge, 1998. This book includes survey chapters for each family, written by experts; it assumes some familiarity with linguistic terminology but will be of use to interested laymen who desire more detail than Dalby, Crystal (1987) or Comrie, Matthews, and Polinsky on this list give in their surveys.

Richardson, David. *Esperanto: Learning and Using the International Language*. El Cerrito, CA: Esperanto League for North America, 1988. This is the best source for learning, or learning about, this fascinating and beautiful experiment.

Rickford, John Russell, and Russell John Rickford. *Spoken Soul: The Story of Black English*. New York: Wiley and Sons, 2000. Most literature on Black English is written from a political and cultural point of view, specifically from the left. This book is no exception, but for those interested in exploring these aspects of the dialect, which will be natural given its charged nature in our times, this book is the most up-to-date and solid and includes some coverage of grammar and history, as well.

Roberts, Peter. *West Indians and Their Language*. Cambridge: Cambridge University Press, 1988. A readable survey of Caribbean creoles, which a great deal of the creolist literature focuses on, despite my aim to give a more global picture in this lecture series. This book also covers the sociological issues that, despite their interest, are not especially germane to the thrust of our story here.

Ruhlen, Merritt. *The Origin of Language: Tracing the Evolution of the Mother Tongue*. New York: John Wiley & Sons, 1994. Merritt Ruhlen and the Proto-World camp's articulate call to arms for the general public. One cannot come away from this book without suspecting that these people are at least on to something.

———. "Taxonomic Controversies in the Twentieth Century," in *New Essays on the Origin of Language*, edited by Jürgen Trabant and Sean Ward, pp. 97–214. Berlin: Mouton de Gruyter, 2001. For those who would like to dig in somewhat more specifically to the Proto-World perspective without being inundated with long lists of words and comparisons only a historical linguist could love, this is the handiest presentation I am aware of.

Sampson, Geoffrey. *Educating Eve: The "Language Instinct" Debate*. London: Cassell, 1997. A gifted rhetorician tears away at the Chomskyan perspective, unique among those making such attempts in having thoroughly engaged the often forbidding literature in question. A valuable counterpoint to Pinker's *The Language Instinct*.

Sebba, Mark. *Contact Languages: Pidgins and Creoles*. New York: St. Martin's Press, 1997. Of the various textbooks on pidgins and creoles, this is the clearest, most up-to-date, and most worldwide in its orientation. Run, don't walk—this one made me decide not to write one of my own.

Simonson, Douglas (Peppo). *Pidgin to da Max*. Honolulu: The Bess Press, 1981. A jocular illustrated glossary of the creole English of Hawaii, focusing on "colorful" vocabulary but giving a good sense of a creole as a living variety.

Stavans, Ilan. *Spanglish: The Making of a New American Language*. New York: HarperCollins, 2003. "Spanglish" has inspired a fair degree of semi-informed musings, but here is finally a more considered and informed piece, also situating the variety sociopolitically.

Thomason, Sarah Grey. *Language Contact: An Introduction*. Washington, DC: Georgetown University Press, 2001. A recent textbook on language mixture—a topic unknown to the textbook until recently—by a linguist with a gift for clarity, as well as relentless good sense. One of my favorite thinkers who has endlessly inspired me—highly recommended.

Versteegh, Kees. *The Arabic Language*. New York: Columbia University Press, 1997. This book includes anything anyone, other than a specialist, would want to know about the awesome cathedral that is Arabic, in accessible language. Details can be bypassed, but this will serve as one's dependable Bible (or Koran) on the subject.

Wallman, Joel. *Aping Language*. Cambridge: Cambridge University Press, 1992. This selection usefully compiles, between two covers, the issues regarding how closely apes approximate human speech. Not too closely, Wallman argues, but the book offers all one needs to know about the field of inquiry as a whole.

Watkins, Calvert, ed. *The American Heritage Dictionary of Indo-European Roots*. Boston: Houghton Mifflin, 1985. This will serve those who want a brass-tacks look at how Indo-Europeanists go about their business. It is a book version of an appendix included in the *American Heritage Dictionary*, aimed at a general readership.

Wells, Spencer. *The Journey of Man: A Genetic Odyssey*. Princeton: Princeton University Press, 2002. An alternative rendition of a story updating Cavalli-Sforza, told more comprehensively by the Oppenheimer book on this list; somewhat lesser on renegade insight and narrative suspense but more compact for those with less time.

Whorf, Benjamin Lee. *Language, Thought, and Reality: Selected Writings of Benjamin Lee Whorf*, edited by J. B. Carroll. Cambridge, MA: MIT Press, 1956. The take-home version of Whorf's ideas on how language channels thought. Now available only at university libraries, but a useful way to get the insights at their source without trawling the obscure and scattered venues in which the work originally appeared.

Wright, Robert. "Quest for the Mother Tongue." *Atlantic Monthly* 267 (1991): 39–68. A general-public account of the Proto-World thesis and its notably acrid reception by most other linguists; this is a nice introduction to whet the appetite for Ruhlen's book.

Internet Resources:

http://www2.arts.gla.ac.uk/IPA/index.html. On the Web site of the International Phonetic Association, you will find charts of the International Phonetic Alphabet, many of whose symbols were used throughout this booklet.

http://www.languagehat.com. A feast for language lovers, consisting of essays, comments, and links to dozens of language-related Web sites, including linguablogs, language resources, and more.

http://www.languagelog.org. A composite of language-related essays; some funny, some serious, all thought-provoking.